GW00496747

Cover design by Spiffing Covers Ltd

ISBN – 978 – 1909425-45-3

This book contains introductory stories which are works of fiction. Names, characters, places and incidents contained within these sections are products of the author's imagination and are used fictitiously. Any resemblance to actual persons, living or dead, or to events or locales is entirely coincidental.

CONTENTS

"Alas for that day!
For the day of the Lord is near;
it will come like destruction from the Almighty."
Joel 1:15[1]
(New International Version)

INTRODUCTION

Elsa's dream

I catch my breath. Illuminated in a beam of light above my bed hovers a paper bird, its translucent wings whirring, pulsing with so much vibrant energy I can almost feel it brush my skin. I love its delicate plumage, its pastel hues of blues, pinks and palest yellow – so exhilarating, so exquisite; it emanates a feeling of such elation and delight that I laugh out loud.

When I wake up for real, my room is filled with sunshine spilling in through the open window, warming my covers, painting my walls with bands of gold, but my beautiful paper bird is gone. Even so, my elated feeling stays with me through the rest of the day.

My dreams don't usually produce that effect when I wake up. I dream I'm running or hiking across country, water skiing behind a snaking motorboat or diving to the depths of the ocean, climbing rugged mountains or dancing and spinning to the gasps of envious spectators. In reality, my legs are useless.

The accident happened almost twenty years ago now. I was only six years old at the time and I have no memory of it. I don't remember much about my life before then either, and, besides, there's not a lot of point in trying. All I know is that I was born with working legs, and maybe that's where my dreams are coming from.

My dad has been amazing, always striving to make things better for me. Nothing but the best is ever good enough. Best education, specialist schools, specialised equipment and so on. He's been tireless. He helped me to learn to do things for myself and to become more independent. It was with his ceaseless encouragement that I took up the kind of sports that are open to wheelers like me. I found I excelled at basketball, and I was chosen to play for the county. I even went snow skiing with some of the team last winter season, which was awesome.

I'm getting worried about my dad, though. I think he's worn himself out. He looks so thin lately, and his energy seems to be slipping away, although he says he's fine. Maybe he overcompensated during all those years because he felt guilty about the accident. Maybe he blames himself for what happened to me and Mom. Like I said, I don't know much about it, but I'm told that Mom was driving the car when it went off the road. It was dark and she didn't see the switchback until it was too late. The car rolled and we wound up at the bottom of a levee. Mom never regained consciousness. Maybe Dad thinks he shouldn't have let her drive on that dangerous road. Anyway, the point is that I think it's time for me to take care of my dad a little more.

We talk about the future sometimes and the prospect of regaining the use of my legs. Recently, we started going to meetings at the Kingdom Hall of Jehovah's Witnesses and we learned about the Bible's

6

promise that when the Day comes, all disabilities will be cured. I love the scripture in Isaiah thirty-five that says, "At that time the lame one will climb up just as a stag does."

We were also shown the story about Jesus when a paralysed man is lowered down to him through the roof of a house. Jesus just says, "Pick up your bed and walk" and the man is cured. This miracle demonstrates that it can be done, and will be done again on a massive scale.

I think about the paper bird; the feeling of weightlessness, the sense of unconfined freedom and happiness it conveyed to me. I don't know why it was made of paper, but I see it as a good thing, a kind of harbinger of hope. I also dream about the resurrection because I will get to meet my mom again and see for myself whether she is as pretty as she looks in the photos. One day we will walk together on a Paradise earth; Mom, Dad, and me without my wheels. Awesome.

***

Although Elsa's story is fictional, it illustrates the fact that Jehovah's Witnesses believe in the resurrection of the dead, not to heavenly life, but to a perfect life on earth, in which there will be no more sickness, old age, or death. Disabled people who live to see that day expect to be made whole, and those who are resurrected expect to be provided with bodies that are free from all physical imperfections.

Today, Jehovah's Witnesses number close to eight million members worldwide. Their peaceful international brotherhood of all races and nationalities is an outstanding achievement. A baptism of total immersion in water is necessary in order to become a dedicated member of Jehovah's Witnesses. It is the outward demonstration of the candidate's commitment to devote the rest of their life to the service of their God, Jehovah. Dedicated Witnesses would describe themselves as Christians, following the highest moral standards; they see themselves as lovers of righteousness, family orientated and law-abiding.

Witnesses do not approve of lying, stealing, gambling or cheating. They do not smoke or take drugs for pleasure, and they do not indulge in drunken behavior. Angry or violent behavior and profanities are not tolerated, neither is racial discrimination. They are exemplary in their honesty.

"An honest person is truthful and free of fraud. He is fair in his dealings with others – straightforward, honorable, not deceptive or misleading. Moreover, an honest person is someone with integrity who does not cheat his fellow man. Honest people contribute to a climate of trust and confidence, which leads to healthy attitudes and promotes strong human relationships."
The Watchtower magazine, November 1, 2000.

These are all qualities that draw people towards the Organization of Jehovah's Witnesses. They are impressed by the fact that Jehovah's Witnesses pride themselves on their strict adherence to such moral principles and guidelines.

Jehovah's Witnesses believe the underlying values come from God and are superior to any other source of information or instruction, but they also believe they are the only religious organization in possession of "the truth," which has set them free from bondage to a wicked world that is alienated from God. Only within the Organization can trustworthy, reliable friends be found. Outside the protection of the Organization they believe that crime and violence are escalating and the world is becoming an increasingly immoral and dangerous place.

Soon, they expect the 'Day of Jehovah' to arrive, during which the earth will be swept clean of most of its inhabitants and all existing governments. Instead, there will be a New World Order under the rule of Christ, who will direct the surviving worldwide Organization of Jehovah's Witnesses. Their existing Governing Body and international organizational structure is viewed as a government-in-waiting for that day.

Common criticisms that they are not Christians, or that they have a different version of the Bible, for example, are untrue. In fact, there are many aspects of Jehovah's Witnesses' lives that differ from the general understanding of them held by the wider community, including some paradoxes that seem inexplicable. Is there more to them than meets the eye?

This book, written from a secular point of view, aims to shed light on the paradox that is Jehovah's Witnesses, digging deeper into their beliefs, moral standards and organizational arrangements. Since Jehovah's Witnesses believe the whole Bible in its entirety to be the inspired word of God, and endeavor to apply its scriptural principles to their lives, many of their practices, for better or for worse, are a natural consequence of this foundation. By exploring their Bible-based approach to life, we are better placed to understand how their reading of the scriptures informs their behavior and their stance on biblical prophecies yet to be fulfilled.

Understanding Jehovah's Witnesses' attitude towards morality and violence is key, but it involves examining unfamiliar territory, parts of the Bible not generally well known but which play a vital part in the formation of their current world view. Only in this way can we begin to understand what makes Jehovah's Witnesses tick.

Our exploration will begin by examining Biblical morality.

MORALITY

Sam supposed he was on the run. An odd expression, when he came to think of it. "On the run" – as if he were confined to an inescapable pathway leading to a single destination. Well, as it happened, it was absolutely true. Of course, they were tracking his vehicle downtown and soon, if he kept going for much longer, he would be intercepted.

Dusk drew down on the city, softening its edges, muting its colors. Massive tower blocks soared overhead like petrified tidal waves glinting in the dying light. Neon signs buried in their depths flashed past in a blur on either side. Sam shook his head in disbelief at the turn events had taken, at the shattered remains of his fractured life.

Realizing he'd missed an instruction, he flung his car to the right, his pickup swaying as he struggled to right it. Cursing under his breath, he pushed his hat to the back of his head and tried to concentrate. Wouldn't do to miss his way now.

Staid. Stolid. Those were the kind of epithets generally linked to his name. His wife was fond of remarking (with more than a hint of sarcasm) that his driving style was sedate. He allowed himself a wry grimace. She should see him now.

"You are nearing your destination," a voice from his dashboard assured him in a tone calculated to induce confidence and a sense of security.

11

This nightmare would be over soon, Sam promised himself. A nightmare that had begun with a note pushed under his door earlier in the evening. He'd recognized his friend's handwriting and taken it inside at once.

"Forgive me for not visiting you in person, old friend. Given my position in central government, it's too risky. I've asked a trusted friend to deliver it because you need to know something. They've done a check on you Sam – the whole 'generation' thing – and they've found something – well, pretty damning. Seems Henry George, your great grandfather, was arrested for the misappropriation of government files – top secret information that nobody was supposed to know about. He was charged with treason and you know what the penalty for that is! Anyway, he had a heart attack and dropped dead two weeks before the tribunal. Need I say more? The fourth generation rule still applies. You're in immediate danger. Get out now, while you still can. – D"

Sam frowned. The old boy had hidden his tracks well enough for his own investigations to turn up nothing significant, but not well enough for the 'Stasi.' What kind of secret information could the government possess that they didn't want to make public? Whatever it was, Henry George hadn't passed his knowledge on – or even the so-called criminal culpability that Sam was supposed to have inherited – but that counted for nothing.

Sam took a left turn, bringing him onto a tree-fringed avenue skirting a broad tidal estuary. Years ago,

12

hundreds of boats lined the jetties, but few could afford them now. The moorings were empty; the jetties were littered with discarded ropes or lay half submerged, their planks rotting.

The 'generation' thing was getting tighter. Tighter governmental control, policing of borders, vetting of populations; it had started with probing checks on immigrants, but genealogy was getting to be a fetish these days. Just about any individual found to have forebears guilty of criminal activity were rooted out, packed off to rehabilitation centers or isolated on penal colonies, depending on the severity of the crime or crimes involved. In the case of forebears convicted of treason or murder, descendents were presumed to have inherited the same criminal tendencies and served with a death sentence. So far, culpability ranged over four generations, but that may well be extended further back in time, the way things were going. Even high-ranking officials were not exempt from the ruling, and some juicy skeletons had popped up in a few unexpected and disturbing places.

A sudden squall of rain spattered the windscreen, sending discarded broadsheets and empty cartons skittering across the highway. Sam ploughed through them, intent on following the route displayed on the dash. It couldn't be much further now. He must see it at any moment.

Pull your vehicle over to the side of the road and await further instructions!

A male voice invaded the interior like a douse of iced water.

Damn! They'd found him already! No, no, no!

Sam checked his visual display and squinted at the road ahead, beads of sweat running down his forehead. He was seconds away. If he could just get there before they cut his engine… A network of girders loomed ahead, their limbs a monstrous ribcage, black against angry clouds tinged with red embers. The bridge!

Sam chuckled as the dash erupted with further staccato directives.

Stop!

Turn around!

Alight from your vehicle now!

This is your last warning!

He could hear sirens. The girders supporting the bridge blurred as he sped even faster, his foot jammed down on the accelerator. He could see lights twinkling on the other side of the estuary.

"Yes!" he breathed, as his dashboard flashed into life once more, eager to keep him informed of his whereabouts.

The tarmac on the bridge, still under construction, fell away beneath him. His vehicle lurched forward and dropped, wheels spinning, as the velvet voice made its final announcement.

"You have reached your destination."

***

14

Crime and punishment

In Exodus chapter twenty, God gave his chosen people ten essential commandments; those he considered to be of the utmost importance. The first of these issues a simple, stern prohibition.

"You must not have any other gods against my face." Exodus 20:3

However, attached to the second commandment, which forbids the carving of false images or idols, is a principle that deserves closer scrutiny.

"... I Jehovah your God am a God exacting exclusive devotion, bringing punishment for the error of fathers upon sons, upon the third generation and upon the fourth generation" Exodus 20:5

This may seem an odd choice of scripture to begin a discussion on Bible morality, but think for a moment about what is actually meant here. It is not about simply allowing the natural consequences of the forefathers' actions to affect their descendents. No, God promises that he is personally "bringing punishment" upon their offspring. Quite a significant distinction. The New International Version renders the same verse,

"You shall not bow down to them or worship them; for I, the LORD your God, am a jealous God, punishing the children for the sin of the parents to the third and fourth generation."

15

Imagine if the government in the country where you live introduced this principle into the justice system. How would you feel if your child were to be tried in court and sentenced to death because of a crime your late grandmother committed? Or if you were to be sentenced to ten years of hard labor because of something your great grandfather did back in the nineteenth century?

What lies at the heart of this scripture is the concept of inherited sin. It is an issue reiterated with considerable force by the Apostle Paul in the New Testament, or Christian Greek Scriptures. Consider the following admonition, set out in his first letter to Timothy.

> *"Let a woman learn in silence with full submissiveness. I do not permit a woman to teach, or to exercise authority over a man, but to be in silence. For Adam was formed first, then Eve. Also, Adam was not deceived, but the woman was thoroughly deceived and came to be in transgression."*
> 1 Timothy 2:11-14

In other words, all women must to be punished for generation upon generation because of something their ancient ancestor, Eve did.

Yet again the same principle is endorsed by the Apostle Paul:

> *"Therefore, just as through one man sin entered into the world, and death through sin, and so death spread to all men, because all sinned."* Romans 5:12

16

The idea of inherited sin is a concept developed by early church fathers, notably Irenaeus, Bishop of Lyons (2nd century, c. AD 202), and Augustine of Hippo (AD 354-430). In Augustine's view, if every individual has innate, inherited sin, then God is justified in hating all humans from birth, and redemption can only be found through Christ.

The damaging moral effect of this doctrine is evident if you observe the actions of people who follow it. It explains why the Israelites thought it was acceptable to kill children in the cities they conquered; their view of justice made children guilty for the sins of their parents. (Deuteronomy 2:34)

The early church fathers applied the same principle to the Jews, whose ancestors were believed to have committed a crime by killing Jesus. Here is John Chrysostom, Archbishop of Constantinople, writing in AD 379:[2]

"The Jews are the most worthless of all men. They are lecherous, rapacious, greedy. They are perfidious murderers of Christ. They worship the Devil. Their religion is a sickness. The Jews are the odious assassins of Christ and for killing God there is no expiation possible, no indulgence or pardon. Christians may never cease vengeance, and the Jew must live in servitude forever. God always hated the Jews. It is essential that all Christians hate them."

The same biblical principle is given expression by Adolf Hitler in April 1933:[3]

> "The Catholic Church considered the Jews pestilent for fifteen hundred years, put them in ghettos, etc., because it recognized the Jews for what they were. In the epoch of liberalism the danger was no longer recognized. I am moving back toward the time in which a fifteen-hundred-year-long tradition was implemented. I do not set race over religion, but I recognize the representatives of this race as pestilent for the state and for the Church, and perhaps I am thereby doing Christianity a great service by pushing them out of schools and public functions."

The holocaust of the Jews is perhaps the most repellent example of what happens when this biblical principle of justice is followed to its logical conclusion. For the Nazis, Jews were deserving of the gas chamber not for what they had personally done wrong, but for who their ancestors were.

Living in the twenty-first century, we should be glad that, with the exception of North Korea,[4] hardly a single country on earth today follows such a principle – not even the Ayatollahs of Iran, the war lords of the Congo, or even the Taliban.

Rights of children

"Happy will he be that grabs ahold and does dash to pieces Your children against the crag." Psalms 137:9

Moral people expect at least minimum standards to be adhered to when it comes to the rights of children. We recognize that children are vulnerable, physically weaker than adults, and need to be protected and able to place their trust in adults without fear of betrayal.

Children's rights include the right to be protected from sexual abuse and exploitation. Children should also be protected from any bad treatment, violence or abuse coming from their parents. They should not be abducted, kidnapped or sold. Minors should not be sent to prison. Minors should not be subject to the death penalty. Finally, children have a right to life, so they should not be murdered or subject to genocide.

The Bible fails to meet these minimum moral standards. Not one clear principle protecting children's rights appears within its pages.

Child abuse has been a serious problem throughout human history, yet God chose not to put anything in the Bible to forbid it. Instead, enshrined in the scriptures are permissions such as this one, enabling a father to sell his daughter as a slave:

> *"And in case a man should sell his daughter as a slave girl, she will not go out in the way that the slave men go out."* Exodus 21:7

In Sodom, when the house at which the patriarch Lot was staying was surrounded by a mob, he was willing to hand his own two daughters over to be gang-raped. No hint of protecting children from sexual abuse appears here:

"Then he said: "Please, my brothers, do not act badly. Please, here I have two daughters who have never had intercourse with a man. Please, let me bring them out to you. Then do to them as is good in your eyes." Genesis 19: 7-8

The context of this scripture well illustrates the Bible's standard of morality. Although Lot is not criticized for his sin, his wife is put to death for the crime of looking behind her. (Genesis 19:26) And while Lot is being protected by God, innocent children are burned to death by the fire and sulphur Jehovah rains down upon them. (Genesis 19: 24-25; 27-29)

Shortly thereafter, the Bible appears to approve of Lot having intercourse with both of his daughters and making them pregnant:

"...and both the daughters of Lot became pregnant from their father." Genesis 19:36

Children and violence

What about the right of children to be free from violent abuse by their parents? Here, the Bible advocates violent discipline:

"Do not hold back discipline from the mere boy. In case you beat him with the rod, he will not die. With the rod you yourself should beat him, that you may deliver his very soul from She'ol itself." Proverbs 23:13,14

Whereas moral principles today safeguard children from the death penalty, Bible morality does not:

"In case a man happens to have a son who is stubborn and rebellious, he not listening to the voice of his father or the voice of his mother, and they have corrected him but he will not listen to them, his father and his mother must also take hold of him and bring him out to the older men of his city and to the gate of his place, and they must say to the older men of his city, 'This son of ours is stubborn and rebellious; he is not listening to our voice, being a glutton and a drunkard.' Then all the men of his city must pelt him with stones, and he must die." Deuteronomy 21:18-21

None of the offenses outlined in this scripture is grave enough to merit a death sentence, but the point here is that the parents are charged with the responsibility of bringing their own son forward for execution.

It is common for children to call others derogatory names sometimes, or to make fun of their elders. It is disrespectful, but it is recognized as a normal but usually fleeting manifestation of childhood behavior. We can be glad that we were not subject to biblical justice as children. Consider the following:

21

"As he [Elisha] was going up on the way, there were small boys that came out from the city and began to jeer him and that kept saying to him: 'Go up, you baldhead! Go up, you baldhead!' Finally he turned behind him and saw them and called down evil upon them in the name of Jehovah. Then two she-bears came out from the woods and went tearing to pieces forty-two children of their number." 2 Kings 2: 23,24

Today, in a moral society, Elisha would receive life imprisonment for the mass murder of these children. Under the Bible's code, his actions were not only approved by God, but he was even revered as a holy prophet. Here, the Bible appears to be more concerned with protecting the adult from children, rather than the other way around.

While moral persons today believe that all children have a right to life, the Bible orders the mass genocide of foreign children, and permits soldiers to take girls as sex slaves (plunder) after winning a battle. Here's another example of an instruction to kill children, this time from Ezekiel:

"And Jehovah went on to say to him: '....Pass through the city after him and strike. Let not your eye feel sorry, and do not feel any compassion. Old man, young man and virgin and little child and women YOU should kill off – to a ruination... Defile the house and fill the courtyards with the slain ones. Go forth!'" Ezekiel 9:5-7

Let's leave the final words on the subject of protecting children with Isaiah:

"Every one that is found will be pierced through, and every one that is caught in the sweep will fall by the sword; and their very children will be dashed to pieces before their eyes. Their houses will be pillaged, and their own wives will be raped." Isaiah 13:15,16

Equality of women

Most people today would agree that women deserve the same inalienable rights as men. We realize that it is not fair to discriminate against women in the workplace, in education, or in the law courts. It is not right to treat women like property to be bought and sold, or to rape them, or take them as sex slaves. These principles are now enshrined in the law of all civilized countries.

The Bible takes a very different stance. In the Old Testament, or Hebrew Scriptures it is acceptable to rape women and take them as sex slaves. (Numbers 31) The Mosaic Law treats women as second-class citizens, the property of men, and it is permitted for men to have more than one wife, as well as concubines; King David had hundreds of wives and concubines. (1 Kings 11:3) King Rehoboam had eighteen wives and sixty concubines, "so that he became father to twenty-eight sons and sixty daughters." (2 Chronicles 11:21) It is also permitted for men to divorce their wives. (Deuteronomy 24:1) The same permissions are not made available to women.

Discrimination against women is embedded deeply in and throughout the Bible. The idea that men may dominate women is established right at the outset.

"To the woman he said: 'I shall greatly increase the pain of your pregnancy; in birth pangs you will bring forth children, and your craving will be for your husband, and he will dominate you.'" Genesis 3:16

In the Mosaic Law, we are given the principle that girl babies are somehow more unclean than boy babies:

"In case a woman conceives seed and does bear a male, she must be unclean seven days. Now if she should bear a female, she must then be unclean fourteen days." Leviticus 12:2;5

If a priest's daughter commits fornication, she must be burned to death.

"Now in case the daughter of a priest should make herself profane by committing prostitution, it is her father that she is profaning. She should be burned in the fire." Levitcus 21:9

No similar punishment is stipulated for a promiscuous son.

The Christian Greek Scriptures continue on the same immoral path with reference to women. I quote once again from the first letter to Timothy on the subject:

24

"Let a woman learn in silence with full submissiveness. I do not permit a woman to teach, or to exercise authority over a man, but to be in silence. For Adam was formed first, then Eve. Also, Adam was not deceived, but the woman was thoroughly deceived and came to be in transgression. However, she will be kept safe through childbearing..." 1 Timothy 2:11-14

This is the scriptural basis for the low status of women within the congregation:

"Let the women keep silent in the congregations, for it is not permitted for them to speak, but let them be in subjection, even as the Law says. If, then, they want to learn something, let them question their own husbands at home, for it is disgraceful for a woman to speak in a congregation." 1 Corinthians 14:34,35

This low opinion of a woman's status emerges again in a letter to the Ephesians:

"Let wives be in subjection to their husbands as to the Lord, because a husband is head of his wife as the Christ also is head of the congregation, he being a savior of [this] body. In fact, as the congregation is in subjection to the Christ, so let wives also be to their husbands in everything." Ephesians 5:22-24

And finally, the most morally repugnant of all:

"For a man ought not to have his head covered, as he is God's image and glory; but the woman is man's glory. For man is not out of woman, but woman out of man; and, what

25

is more, man was not created for the sake of the woman, but woman for the sake of the man." 1 Cor. 11:7-9

Woman is created "for the sake of the man." This scripture is the rationale for rape, the taking of sex slaves, bigamy, the treating of women as property, and the low status of women in society. As a result of following these biblical passages, a catalog of abuse has been directed against women throughout the ages. Women have been excluded from education, banned from attending university, prevented from developing a career and denied voting rights as responsible citizens. They have been sold as goods, treated as possessions, and not even allowed ownership of their own children or their own home. They have suffered and continue to suffer physical and mental abuse.

All the discrimination, heartache, and pain could have been avoided if only God had penned a simple moral principle to be included in the Bible – that women are equal and have equal rights.

Today, the same attitude towards women can be seen in those countries that still apply Biblical Law (including Muslim countries, as Muslims also accept the first five books of the Bible); countries such as Yemen, Pakistan, Saudi Arabia, Iran, Uzbekistan, and Afghanistan. In Saudi Arabia women, despite owning real estate as well as managing their own businesses, are sexually segregated, restricted to "appropriate" professions, and not allowed to drive a car or to vote.

In Yemen the minimum marriage age of fifteen for women has been abolished and the onset of puberty, sometimes taken to be as low as the age of nine, is now the standard criterion used to indicate eligibility for marriage.

Meanwhile, in Afghanistan and in some areas of Pakistan, the Taliban has forced professional women to give up their jobs and prohibited girls from attending school. At the time of writing, fifteen-year-old schoolgirl and education campaigner, Malala Yousafzai has made a remarkable recovery in hospital in Britain after being shot in the head by Taliban militants in north-western Pakistan for promoting the right of girls in that country to go to school.

Slavery

What moral guidelines does the Bible give on the subject of slavery?

> "In assessing the moral wisdom of the Bible, it is useful to consider moral questions that have been solved to everyone's satisfaction. Consider the question of slavery. The entire civilized world now agrees that slavery is an abomination. What moral instruction do we get from the God of Abraham on this subject? Consult the Bible, and you will discover that the creator of the universe clearly expects us to keep slaves." [5]

In the third book of the Bible, Leviticus, God gives his chosen people this advice:

27

"As for your slave man and your slave girl who become yours -"

- you must set them free?

"- from the nations that are round about you people, from them you may buy a slave man and a slave girl. And also from the sons of the settlers who are residing as aliens with you, from them you may buy, and from their families that are with you whom they had born to them in your land; and they must become your possession. And you must pass them on as an inheritance to your sons after you to inherit as a possession to time indefinite. You may use them as workers, but upon your brothers the sons of Israel, you must not tread, the one upon the other, with tyranny." Leviticus 25:44-46

Notice that slavery is only considered a tyranny when it comes to treating fellow Israelites in that way.

Advocates of the traffic in black slaves from Africa's Ivory Coast justified their actions by quoting from the Bible's book of Genesis,

"Cursed be Canaan. Let him become the lowest slave to his brothers." - Genesis 9:25

This Bible's principle of inherited sin was used by them to claim that black people were descendents of the Canaanites and therefore they had a God-given right to use them as slaves. It was the rationale used in South

Africa for their divisive Apartheid policy, and was taught from the pulpit of the Dutch Reformed Church in that country.

Mormons believed that the mark God set upon Cain after he slew his brother was black skin, leading them to forbid black people from entering the Mormon priesthood, a rule that was only repealed in 1978. (Genesis 4:15 KJV)

The treatment of slaves is not forgotten in the Christian Greek Scriptures. Rather than dispensing new light on the subject, encouraging Christians to give slaves their freedom, Paul recommends that slaves should cultivate the following attitude:

"You slaves be obedient to those who are your masters in a fleshly sense, with fear and trembling in the sincerity of your hearts, as to the Christ." Eph. 6:5

His first letter to Timothy contains similar admonition.

"Let as many as are slaves under a yoke keep on considering their owners worthy of full honor, that the name of God and the teaching may never be spoken of injuriously." 1 Timothy 6:1

The Christian Greek Scriptures constitute a lost opportunity to introduce higher standards of equality. Instead, the practice of slavery was able to continue relatively unchecked long after the Bible's publication and distribution throughout the civilized world. It was not until the nineteenth century that increasing criticism of the practice by concerned individuals and groups led to its eventual abolition. Even though slavery continues to exist in one form or another, it has now been declared immoral and illegal in all nations of the world.

The United Nations Universal Declaration of Human Rights states simply,

"No one shall be held in slavery or servitude; slavery and the slave trade shall be prohibited in all their forms." Article 4

Just a few succinct words of similar condemnation in the Bible might have ended it a great deal sooner for many thousands of enslaved peoples.

The right to a fair and independent trial

In the secular world, biblical law was superseded by the introduction of trial by jury, introduced in England during the reign of Henry II to replace religious trial by 'ordeals.' [6] It was later enshrined in the Magna Carta – one of the most important historical documents in medieval history – signed in the year 1215. Moral societies recognize the right of each individual, when accused of wrongdoing, to a fair, impartial, and independent trial. The principle is clear that a person is innocent until proven guilty. Punishment must not be given until after guilt has been established.

Magna Carta panel, Canterbury pulpit,- Washington National
Cathedral, Washington DC
Source: www.flickr.com. Tim Evanson, Sept. 2012

In modern, democratic countries the system of law grants
those charged with a criminal offense the opportunity to
defend themselves, and they have the right to legal
representation. Representation is considered essential,
regardless of status. In the UK, if an accused person is not
able to afford the fee of a professional lawyer, one is
provided at the government's expense.

Because individuals are generally not capable of being
objective when in dispute with someone else, there must
be a clear separation between those who govern on the
one hand and the judiciary (the court system) on the other.
An independent court system prevents a person in a
position of power from bending the judicial system to his
own will, or using it to persecute those he considers his
enemies. The court system ensures that independent,

impartial jury members, who are not personally involved in any way in the dispute, make the judgements.

All civilized countries of the world follow this system. Those countries that ignore these principles are without exception miserable places, where life is brutally unfair, whose people are condemned to live in abject poverty, and where life is cheap.

The Bible does not recognize any of the principles of civilized countries. You can see this in the instructions given in Deuteronomy 21 concerning the rebellious son quoted earlier, where the death sentence is advocated. Let's analyze it in a little more detail:

"In case a man happens to have a son who is stubborn and rebellious, he not listening to the voice of his father or the voice of his mother, and they have corrected him but he will not listen to them, his father and his mother must also take hold of him and bring him out to the older men of his city and to the gate of his place, and they must say to the older men of his city, 'This son of ours is stubborn and rebellious; he is not listening to our voice, being a glutton and a drunkard.' Then all the men of his city must pelt him with stones, and he must die." Deuteronomy 21:18-21

Note that there is no independent jury. No opportunity is provided for the son to defend himself against the allegations, or to call witnesses, nor is he given access to someone who can speak in his defense. The people making the decision are "the older men of his city." In other words, they are the same people who are governing the city – they are not independent and should not be in a position to make a judgement on the case.

The Bible does state that there must be at least two witnesses to a crime before the accused can be executed, which provides some protection, but is not proof against unscrupulous attempts to discredit the accused, or to use them as 'scapegoats' for the crimes of others.

"In case there should be found in your midst in one of your cities that Jehovah your God is giving you a man or a woman who should practice what is bad in the eyes of Jehovah your God so as to overstep his covenant, and he should go and worship other gods and bow down to them or to the sun or the moon or all the army of the heavens, a thing that I have not commanded, and it has been told you and you have heard it and have searched thoroughly, and, look! the thing is established as the truth, this detestable thing has been done in Israel! you must also bring that man or that woman who has done this bad thing out to your gates, yes, the man or the woman, and you must stone such one with stones, and such one must die. At the mouth of two witnesses or of three witnesses the one dying should be put to death." Deuteronomy 17:2-6

Again there is no independent jury, no independent judge, no defense lawyer, no chance for the man or the woman to defend themselves, or call witnesses on their behalf, and no trial. Once again, the morality of the Bible falls far below that of the contemporary world.

At least in the two cases quoted above there was a process of sorts, but often no such process is in evidence. The Bible is full of summary executions without trial, like that of Lot's wife. (Genesis 19:24-26)

The right to freedom of belief

As humans, we struggle to make sense of our world. On almost every topic you can think of there are many different points of view, all sincerely held. That is why moral people uphold the principle of the freedom of belief. The Universal Declaration of Human Rights puts it this way:

"Everyone has the right to freedom of thought, conscience and religion; this right includes freedom to change his religion or belief, and freedom, either alone or in community with others and in public or private, to manifest his religion or belief in teaching, practice, worship and observance."
Article 18

Biblical morality does not uphold this standard:

"One who sacrifices to any gods but Jehovah alone is to be devoted to destruction." Exodus 22:20

"Furthermore, they entered into a covenant... that anyone that would not search for Jehovah the God of Israel should be put to death, whether small or great, whether man or woman." Chronicles 15:12,13

34

"In case you hear it said in one of your cities, which Jehovah your God is giving you to dwell there, 'Good-for-nothing men have gone out from your midst that they may try to turn away the inhabitants of their city, saying: "Let us go and serve other gods," whom you have not known,' you must also search and investigate and inquire thoroughly; and if the thing is established as the truth, this detestable thing has been done in your midst, you should without fail strike the inhabitants of that city with the edge of the sword. Devote it and everything that is in it, and its domestic animals, to destruction at the edge of the sword." Deuteronomy 13:12-15

The above standards of biblical morality are still applied in several countries to this day, with vile consequences. Religious dissent in the form of blasphemy or apostasy can be punished with the death penalty in at least seven countries: Egypt, Iran, Libya, Pakistan, Saudi Arabia, Sudan, and Afghanistan. The Bureau of Consular Affairs in the United States warns citizens traveling to Afghanistan,

"Afghan law carries a maximum penalty of death for those charged with proselytizing, if convicted. Evidence may consist of possession of non-Islamic religious material, especially in local languages. Allegations of conversion of Afghan citizens are taken particularly seriously. The testimony of three individuals or a group is enough to convict someone of proselytizing. The same penalty exists in law for Afghan citizens who convert to

35

another religion. All Afghan citizens are considered Muslim from birth. Converts are subject to arrest regardless of where the conversion took place, and Afghan-U.S. dual nationals are also subject to this law." [7]

The death penalty for blasphemy also exists in Pakistan. Even though no one has yet been executed officially for blasphemy in Pakistan, there have been reports of "mob lynchings and widespread mistreatment of those accused."[8] A recent case in August 2012 drew international concern. Riftah Masih, an eleven-year-old Christian Pakistani girl was arrested, imprisoned, and faced a possible death penalty after she was accused of blasphemy for allegedly burning pages of the Q'uran, despite the fact that it could not be established if she herself had committed the offense. She has since been released on $10,000 bail, to an uncertain future.

The Death Penalty

How do you feel when you read reports like these, coming from Iran?

Alireza Molla Soltani was hanged in a public execution on 21 September 2011, aged 17 years old.

Delara Darabi was hanged in May 2009, age 22, for a crime she allegedly committed when she was 17.

Atefeh Sahaaleh Rajabi was executed on 15 August 2004 by hanging. Her execution was conducted in a public square in the small tourist city of Neka, Iran. She was just 16 years old.

There are currently one hundred juveniles on death row also awaiting execution. 'Safe World for Women' explains how this situation is possible.

"Section 26 of the Islamic Penal Code of Iran protects children from legal liability, holding their parent or guardian responsible 'for their correction under the supervision of the court.' However, it also considers girls criminally responsible at age 9 and boys at age 15. So children may be imprisoned until they reach age 18, at which time the sentence is carried out." [9]

Even so, according to Amnesty International, Iran has executed forty-three juveniles under the age of eighteen since 2004, including two juveniles hanged on 20th April 2011.

We have already seen how often the Bible calls for the death penalty. In the world today, relatively few developed countries retain capital punishment. Those countries that do retain it are generally marked by a higher murder rate, poverty, and social deprivation. The United States is the exception in this list, though it too suffers a higher rate of murder and violent crime compared to countries that have abolished the death penalty.

While reading through the following list of countries, ask yourself how many of these countries you would like to take up permanent residence in. Countries allowing the death penalty as of March 2012, according to Amnesty International, are:[10]

Afghanistan	China	Guyana	Lebanon	Saint Lucia	Trinidad and Tobago
Antigua and Barbuda	Comoros	India	Lesotho	Saint Vincent & Grenadines	Uganda
Bahamas	Congo (Democratic Republic)	Indonesia	Libya	Saudi Arabia	United Arab Emirates
Bahrain	Cuba	Iran	Malaysia	Singapore	United States
Bangladesh	Dominica	Iraq	Nigeria	Somalia	Vietnam
Barbados	Egypt	Jamaica	Oman	South Sudan	Yemen
Belarus	Equatorial Guinea	Japan	Pakistan	Sudan	Zimbabwe
Belize	Ethiopia	Jordan	Palestinian Authority	Syria	
Botswana	Guatemala	North Korea	Qatar	Taiwan	
Chad	Guinea	Kuwait	Saint Kitts & Nevis	Thailand	

Capital crimes in the Bible

Below is a list of twenty-four 'crimes' for which the Bible imposes the death penalty. As you read through the list, again ask yourself whether you would like to live in a country with these rules on its statute books – a country where you or your loved ones could be accused of one of these crimes at any time, without the right to a fair trial, and without access to a defense lawyer or an impartial jury.

- Holding beliefs that differ from those of the government (apostasy)
- Living in a town where someone else holds a belief different from that of the presiding government – Deuteronomy 13:12-15
- Failing to get circumcised – Genesis 17:14
- Looking back when told not to – Genesis 19:26
- Hitting your father or mother – Exodus 21:15
- Owning a bull that gores somebody, after failing to pen it up properly – Exodus 21:28
- Eating leavened bread during the festival of unleavened bread – Exodus 12:15
- Manufacturing unauthorised anointing oil – Exodus 30:33
- Eating quails – Numbers 11:31-35
- Picking up sticks on the Sabbath - Numbers 15:32-36
- Other forms of working on the Sabbath – Exodus 31:12-15
- Waiting too long before eating sacrificial meat – Leviticus 19:5-8
- Cursing your father or mother – Leviticus 20:9

- Having sexual relations with your father's secondary wife (not your mother) – Leviticus 20:20
- Spilling semen on the ground during intercourse – Genesis 38:9,10
- Sexual intercourse with your wife while she is menstruating – Leviticus 20:18
- Being a victim of rape in a city but not crying out loud enough for help – Deuteronomy 22:23-27
- Not being a virgin (applies to women only) on your wedding night – Deuteronomy 22:13-21
- Not listening to a priest or judge – Deuteronomy 17:12
- Blasphemy – Leviticus 24:10-16
- Being a stubborn or rebellious child – Deuteronomy 21:18-21
- Perjury – Deuteronomy 19:15-21
- Living in a country where the government decides to conduct a census – 2 Samuel 24:15
- Being descended from anyone who committed any of the above – Exodus 20:5.

In contrast, have a look at an equally extensive list of *permitted* behavior, bringing no punishment at all, according to the Bible's morality. How would you like to live in a country where any these things are practiced by your neighbors?

- Mass genocide of foreigners, including women and children – Joshua 10 and 11
- Assaulting foreigners for the purpose of taking their women and girls as sex slaves – Judges 21

- Harboring racist attitudes, calling foreigners 'dogs' – Matthew 15:24-26
- Refusing to let your child marry a foreigner – Deuteronomy 7:3-4; Nehemiah 13:23-27
- Honor killing of all the inhabitants of an entire town because one of the men there slept with your sister – Genesis 34:25-29
- Killing all the inhabitants of a city because some of their number did not agree with your preaching – Matthew 10:14,15
- Human trafficking; buying, selling, and owning slaves – Leviticus 25:44-46
- Selling your own daughter as a slave – Exodus 21:8
- Having sex with your own child – Genesis 19:30-36
- Handing your daughter over to an angry mob to be gang-raped – Genesis 19:6-8
- Beating your child – Proverbs 23:14, 15
- Killing your own son because he is disrespectful – Deuteronomy 21:18-21
- Killing young boys because they called you names – 2 Kings 2:23,24
- Sleeping with a prostitute – Genesis 38:14-18
- Having more than one wife at a time – 1 Kings 11:3
- Having concubines in addition to multiple wives – 2 Samuel 3:7; Esther 2:12-14;
- Having the right to divorce any wife at a whim – Deuteronomy 24:1
- Refusing to let your wife speak in public – 1 Cor. 14:34,35
- Discriminating against women in all walks of life – 1 Cor. 11:9

- Publicly humiliating a colleague and friend – Gal. 2:11-14
- Killing anyone who has a different religion to your own – Matthew 7:15-20.

The above examples are by no means exhaustive. The Bible is bristling with examples of behavior and principles fully endorsed by God that most people today would find immoral and offensive.

To illustrate this kind of moral reversal, let's see how it operates using the example of Judah and his daughter-in-law, Tamar, found in Genesis 38.

1. Tamar's husband is executed by God without trial, for no reason other than because God disliked him. This is *not* considered immoral. (verse 7)
2. Judah asks another son of his (Onan) to have intercourse with Tamar so that she can have a child. This part is also *not* considered immoral. (We are not told how Onan's wife felt about this arrangement.) (verse 8)
3. Onan spills his semen on the ground. This *is* considered immoral, and for this crime Onan is instantly executed without trial. (verse 9)
4. Later Judah sees a prostitute and pays her for sex. This is *not* considered immoral. (verses 14-18)
5. However the prostitute turns out to be Tamar in disguise, and she conceives a child. (verse 19) When Judah finds out that Tamar has been a

prostitute he immediately orders her to be executed (without trial) by burning her alive. This part is *not* viewed as immoral. (verse 24)

6. Finally Tamar reveals that she is the same prostitute that Judah had sex with, so he spares her. (verses 25-26)

7. Tamar gives birth to a son, Perez (verse 29) who is later identified as an ancestor of Jesus (Luke 3:33), thus implying that this whole episode was part of God's plan, and therefore is *not* considered immoral.

At every stage of the above events, the concepts 'moral' and 'immoral' are exactly reversed.

Why do Jehovah's Witnesses not see the immorality of these principles? The answer is that they believe the Bible to be the literal word of God. Where biblical morality goes against their conscience, they will, without exception, follow the Bible rather than their conscience every time.

Some will observe that in this chapter I have focussed on the negative aspects of the Bible's morality, and have left out all that is positive. Certainly it would be wrong to deny that there are many admirable sentiments expressed in the Bible, such as the principle to treat others as we would like to be treated ourselves, for those without sin to "cast the first stone" (John 8:7); not to steal and cheat; to be humble, unselfish, and to help others in need. There are

43

passages in the book of Psalms and the Song of Solomon that are poetic and lyrical. Countless people draw comfort and inspiration from positive aspects of the Bible. In reality, the Bible simply reflects human nature, the good and bad, encapsulating morality as it was in the ancient societies that practiced it.

Christendom today tends to focus on the more positive aspects of the Bible and plays down or ignores the scenes of violence and immorality. Thus, it has had a benign impact on much of our modern culture. Many Christians distance themselves from Jehovah, the "manly person of war" striding through the pages of the Old Testament. (Exodus 15:3) Jehovah's Witnesses, on the other hand, are very much concerned with worshiping the God of the Israelites by name and familiarising themselves with his exploits. My point is that instead of accepting the bad for what it is, these champions of Jehovah rationalize and sanction the immorality we have seen displayed in the Bible because they believe it bears the stamp of their God's approval. As a result, they are negatively influenced by it. Simply stated, you need look no further than the name they have chosen for themselves, "Jehovah's Witnesses" in order to identify their chosen moral standards.

As we shall see in later chapters, Jehovah's Witnesses allow questionable morals in Bible stories to influence their organization, the structure of their society, and their way of life. They instill these stories into the minds and hearts of their children from birth, in obedience to the scripture at Deuteronomy 6 verse 7:

"And these words that I am commanding you today must prove to be on your heart; and you must inculcate them into your son and speak of them when you sit in your house and when you walk on the road and when you lie down and when you get up."

Witness children grow up with literature written specifically for them, such as, 'My Book of Bible Stories,' which is illustrated with many of the violent incidents in the Hebrew scriptures, including Abraham's willingness to kill his own son, the storm of fire and brimstone that God rains down upon Sodom and Gomorra, and the drowning of the Egyptians and their horses in the Red Sea.

After the Day of Jehovah, Jehovah's Witnesses expect to set up a global government following many of the same biblical morals and principles we have discussed in this chapter, but implemented worldwide.

VIOLENCE

A hot sun beat down upon the sloping meadows, pasturelands and plum orchards of the Visegrad valley, heating the red tiled roofs of abandoned farmhouses and exposing in sharp relief the suppurating sores of the civil war in Bosnia; unexploded cluster bombs, shrapnel-shattered houses and a steady exodus of displaced refugees.

Sanja sat in the shade cast by a spreading beech tree, while two women tended her wounds as best they could, flicking away the flies that swarmed incessantly beneath the leafy canopy. Sanja's body was covered with burns. Ugly black scabs covered her face, her lips were cracked and blistered and her ears all but melted away. Her hands and feet were a mass of seared flesh. She was well aware that infection had already set in.

The doctor was less kind than the women. "I cannot waste these precious medicines on you," he told her. "You will not survive."

"I will," she whispered fiercely, her throat still raw. "Please, I must!"

Behind him, she was dimly aware of a slim figure striding rapidly towards her. He wore light-colored trousers and an open-necked shirt, a leather bag slung casually across his shoulders. A foreigner, perhaps an

46

Englishman. The doctor, having noticed the stranger at the same time, reluctantly parted with some of the precious antibiotics he carried with him and took his leave.

The young man approached her, pulling off his wide-brimmed hat, and introduced himself.

"Peter Delgado, war correspondent for the *Daily Telegraph*," he announced. "I heard there was a survivor of the Bikavac fire. It took me some time to find you. Are you able to talk?"

Sanja nodded. She had not spoken to anyone yet. Who was there left? She stared at him. The journalist had an earnest face and keen, soft eyes that promised truth and fidelity. She nodded. She would tell him her story.

"We were together in the house; my mother, my two sisters and our four children," she began, her voice no more than a whisper, but strangely powerful. "We were afraid, terrified of what was going to happen next. Our menfolk had disappeared, we did not know where, but we heard there was a massacre on the Drina Bridge in Visegrad – men, with their hands tied behind their backs, their throats cut like cattle, hurled into the river." She shuddered, her breath catching in her throat. "We had also heard that hundreds of young women were herded into the town spa and raped."

The young journalist said nothing, but he had heard accounts of these very atrocities from the lips of refugees fleeing Visegrad. He had wondered whether they were true, or simply wartime propaganda. Now he felt certain

47

they must have happened. He poured Sanja a glass of water, leaning forward to place it in her burned and bandaged hands. She winced as the glass pressed down on her wounds.

"We thought perhaps Bikavac would not be so bad. It is only a small village and everybody knows each other there. Christian and Muslim families have grown up together. There did not seem to be any animosity between us. But then there was a knock on the door." She paused, reliving the moment. The journalist touched her arm gently.

"You're doing well," he murmured. "Take as much time as you want."

"It was Redzic," she whispered, her glass trembling in her hand, slopping the water over the side and soaking through her stained bandages.

Jusuf Redzic. A Serbian policeman now, but she had known him since high school. Surely he would not harm them?

"Sanja Prazina, you must come with me," he had ordered, adding with a sweeping glance, "all of you." She had examined his face, the expression in his eyes as he herded them out of the house, refusing to allow them to collect any of their possessions. He was like a stranger.

"Jusuf took us to another house further along the road where we could see Serb men pushing more women and small children inside," she continued. 'Don't worry,' I told my mother, 'they won't kill us!' but then I saw there was a wardrobe against the front door and all the

48

windows outside had been blocked with furniture. The men started throwing stones at us, and then hand grenades. The women were screaming and the children were crying. We were the last ones in. There must have been sixty or seventy of us. Then they set the house on fire."

She gasped, sucking in the burning air again, choking on the acrid smoke, her ears filled with terrified screams and the roar of crackling flames. She shook her head and rocked herself backwards and forwards.

"I saw a window in the garage door," she rasped. "I was the only one who got out... The children, my little one..." She made a harsh sound like a sob. "As I ran, I pulled off my burning clothes. Outside, Chetniks [Serb nationalists] were standing around watching the house burn. They were playing music very, very loudly, so no one could hear the sounds of the burning people screaming inside."

***

The above story is based closely on the experience of a Muslim woman, Zehra Turjacanin, the sole survivor of the Bikavac fire in 1992, taken from a report by Alec Russell, war correspondent on the Bosnian war, entitled 'Unforgiven, Unforgotten, Unresolved. Bosnia,' printed in the *FT Weekend* magazine, March 24/25, 2012. I relate it here because it is doubtful that anybody would have difficulty in describing this horrific event as an atrocity. In fact, the Bikavac fire remains one of the worst single atrocities of the Bosnian war.

When Jehovah's Witnesses are presented with contemporary accounts of ethnic cleansing, like the Bikavac fire, they are as outraged as everyone else, but when such atrocities are set within a biblical context – atrocities just as horrific as those in Bosnia – they see nothing wrong in them. On the contrary, they draw freely from these biblical sources, often presenting them in a positive light.

The Apostle Paul's second letter to Timothy makes the statement,

> "All scripture is inspired of God and beneficial for teaching, for reproving, for setting things straight, for disciplining in righteousness, that the man of God may be fully competent, completely equipped for every good work." 2 Timothy 3:16

Jehovah's Witnesses believe this statement to be true. 'Read God's Word the Holy Bible Daily,' appears in huge letters above one of the Watchtower Bible and Tract Society's buildings at Brooklyn, New York. Witnesses are encouraged to view the scriptures as "spiritual food," to be partaken of on a regular basis. We have already seen what it has to say on issues of morality. Now we need to find out what attitude God's chosen people, the Israelites, took towards violence. We must also examine the New Testament, or Christian Greek Scriptures to discover whether it sheds new light on issues of violence. Taken together, have the Hebrew and Greek scriptures proved to be a positive influence on human behavior?

In the name of God

- May 13, 2005, in the city of Andijan, twenty-three imprisoned businessmen were freed by their supporters. A meeting was then held in the town square, where an estimated 10,000 people gathered, who expected government officials to come and listen to their grievances. Instead, Islam Karimov sent in the Uzbekistan army. They massacred hundreds of innocent men, women, and children.

- In 2005, Robert Mugabe launched Operation Murambatsvina (Clean the Filth), forcibly evicting some 700,000 people from their homes and businesses in Zimbabwe — ostensibly "to restore order and sanity."

- Since February 2003, Omar el-Bashir's campaign of ethnic and religious persecution has killed at least 180,000 civilians in Darfur in western Sudan and driven 2 million people from their homes.

- In Iran, the country is run by a small Guardian Council, overseen by the Ayatollah Khamane'i, which has the right to veto any law that the elected government passes. Khamane'i has closed down the free press, tortured journalists, and ordered the execution of homosexual males.[11]

Here again, individuals presented with the above facts have no difficulty recognizing them as abuses of human rights. Yet, when it comes to the Bible, Jehovah's Witnesses and many other fundamentalist Christians lay aside their sense of injustice and generally condone the very things they condemn in modern day tyrants and dictators.

Take the systematic genocide and ethnic cleansing that was carried out on a grand scale in the so-called "promised land" of Israel as an example; men, women, and children dispossessed of the land they had cultivated for generations, and slaughtered in their thousands by the militant Israelites. (Numbers 21:31-35; Deuteronomy 2:34; Deuteronomy 7:1-5) What could possibly persuade an individual or group of peace-loving people to consider such brutality acceptable? What is the rationale compelling them to endorse such acts of violence? Also, what are the implications involved in cultivating such an attitude?

In the eyes of Jehovah's Witnesses, acts of ethnic cleansing and rapine carried out by the ancient Israelites are acceptable to them, despite their paradoxical belief in peace, because they were carried out in the name of God. Since God told them to do it, the reasoning goes, it must be acceptable.

The Israelites believed that cleansing the land of worshipers of other gods would make it a better place for their own people. But from the point of view of the orthodox Christians who carried out ethnic cleansing and acts of rape in Bosnia, they too were worshipers of the God of the Bible, acting on the belief that in order to create a better and more just future for their people, they needed to cleanse their country of the worshipers of Allah. Considered objectively, is there any moral difference between these acts of aggression?

War against the Midianites

Keep in mind the atrocities committed against the Muslim women of Bosnia as you follow the events recorded in Numbers chapter 31. We take up the account after the Israelites waged war with the Midianites, executing their kings, and slaughtering all males without mercy.

> *"But the sons of Israel carried off the women of Midian and their little ones captive, and all their domestic animals and all their livestock and all their means of maintenance they plundered. And all their cities in which they had settled and all their walled camps they burned with fire."* Numbers 31:9,10

It is almost impossible to imagine the devastation of such a war. Not only are all Midianite men put to death, regardless of age or infirmity, but the women and children are "carried off." What might this mean? There is no indication that the women and their children are kept together or that the Midianite women are allowed to continue caring for their offspring. They are now captives,

53

their homes destroyed, forced to accompany the men that have murdered their fathers, brothers, husbands, and sons.

It beggars belief that the devastation the Israelites brought to bear upon the Midianites was still not thorough enough for Moses. He grew highly indignant with his combat chiefs because they spared the lives of all the women and children.

> *"Have you preserved alive every female?" he raged, "...And now kill every male among the little ones, and kill every woman who has had intercourse with a man by lying with a male. And preserve alive for yourselves all the little ones among the women who have not known the act of lying with a male."* Numbers 31:14,17

If you were to ask one of Jehovah's Witnesses, or indeed many Christians, if they believe Moses was a moral man, they would answer in the affirmative. They accept the Bible's description of him as, *"by far the meekest of all the men who were upon the surface of the ground."* (Numbers 12:3) He is viewed as a shining example of faithfulness, loyalty, and obedience to the will of God. Yet not only did Moses approve of the mass murder of Midianite adult civilians, but he demanded that the Israelites seize all their children, infants, and virgin women. The Bible does not give details as to how such a humiliating check on virginity was carried out, but its purpose must have struck terror into their hearts. Any surviving Midianite women who were identified as not being virgins were to be executed. We are left to guess how those who stood condemned were killed. Put to the sword maybe? Or forced into a building and burned alive?

But why kill only the women who were not virgins? For what purpose could virgin girls be kept alive? Verse 26 describes them as 'booty.' What possible function could a virgin female perform as 'booty' that a non-virgin female could not?

The Benjamites' dilemma

Further insight into the Bible's attitudes towards violence can be found in Judges 20 and 21:10-25, which is worth examining in some detail. In chapter 20, one of the twelve tribes of Israel, the Benjamites, disgrace themselves in the eyes of the other tribes, because certain men in the Benjamite city of Gibeah have abused and raped the concubine of a Levite man visiting the city. The Levite finds her dead body on his doorstep in the morning, so he takes a knife and proceeds to carve her body up into twelve parts and send them to all the tribes of Israel, demanding justice. In retaliation, the Israelites launch an attack on the Benjamites and slaughter all the men, women, children, and animals in their towns and cities, just as they did with the Midianites.

"The men of Israel went back to Benjamin and put all the towns to the sword, including the animals and everything

else they found. All the towns they came across they set on fire." Judges 20:48:

Having carried out this bloody rampage to their satisfaction, the Israelites now mourn the fact that the tribe of Benjamin is cut off from Israel. Belatedly, they wonder how wives can be provided for the surviving Benjamite males, since the Israelites themselves have sworn never to give their own women to them as wives. Fortunately, a solution presents itself to them. They discover that none of the people from Jabesh Gilead have come to attend an assembly to make burnt offerings to God. Judges 21 Verses 10-12 takes up the account.

"Hence the assembly proceeded to send twelve thousand of the most valiant men there and to command them saying: 'Go, and you must strike the inhabitants of Jabesh-gilead with the edge of the sword, even the women and the little ones. And this is the thing that you should do: Every male and every woman that has experienced lying with a male you should devote to destruction.' However, they found out of the inhabitants of Jabesh-gilead four hundred girls, virgins that had not had intercourse with a man by lying with a male. So they brought them to the camp at Shiloh, which is in the land of Canaan."

The Israelites are now in a position to pardon the Benjamites, giving them the captured virgins from Jabesh Gilead as a peace offering to welcome them back into the fold. Yet there is still a problem. There are not enough

56

women for all of the Benjamite males. (Judges 21:13,14) How do the Israelites address this shortfall?

"Finally they said: 'Look! There is a festival of Jehovah from year to year in Shiloh, which is to the north of Bethel, toward the east of the highway that goes up from Bethel to Shechem and toward the south of Lebonah.'

"So they commanded the sons of Benjamin, saying: 'Go, and you must lie in wait in the vineyards. And you must look, and, there now, when the daughters of Shiloh come on out to dance in circle dances, you must also come out from the vineyards and carry off for yourselves by force each one his wife from the daughters of Shiloh, and you must go to the land of Benjamin.

"Accordingly the sons of Benjamin did just that way, and they proceeded to carry off wives for their number from the women dancing around, whom they snatched away; after which they went off and returned to their inheritance and built the cities and took up dwelling in them." (Judges 21 verses 19-21, 23)

Restated, the Israelites begin a campaign of vengeance by murdering thousands of innocent people living in Benjamite towns who probably knew little or nothing about the original reason for the conflict. Notice also that once again in Judges 21:10-12 there is the same practice of examining women to see who is a virgin and killing all the rest, then taking the virgins as sex slaves.

Not content with the gift of captured women from Jabeth Gilead, the Benjamites – with full encouragement from the other tribes – hide beside the road and kidnap the young women of Shiloh to make up the shortfall, carrying them off "by force." These hapless victims are termed euphemistically, "wives," but there is no doubt that these women were raped, then forced to live with these men and bear their children.

Surely, if a Benjamite raped the Levite man's concubine in Gibeah, the perpetrator should have been sought out and brought to justice. Instead, the Israelites turned it into an occasion for a vengeful massacre. You might expect a just God to be angry with his people for committing such atrocities, but there is no hint of condemnation in the biblical account.

The deluge

Moving on, the story of the Flood is well known, but for Jehovah's Witnesses, it prefigures the coming day of "the wrath of God the Almighty" at Armageddon. (Revelation 19:15) You can read a description of the Flood in the Bible at Genesis, chapters six to eight, but I think it's worth recounting here the consequences of God's act of divine justice. (Genesis 7:21-24)

"So all flesh that was moving upon the earth expired, among the flying creatures and among the domestic animals and among the wild beasts and among all the swarms that were swarming upon the earth, and all mankind. Everything in

which the breath of the force of life was active in its nostrils, namely, all that were on the dry ground, died. Thus he wiped out every existing thing that was on the surface of the ground, from man to beast, to moving animal and to flying creature of the heavens, and they were wiped off the earth; and only Noah and those who were with him in the ark kept on surviving."

Fundamentalist Christians, including Jehovah's Witnesses, accept the Flood as a factual account of what actually took place 'in the days of Noah.' Therefore, assuming it is truthful, and taking Bible chronology at face value, only 2,000 years had passed since God created human life on Earth. Now here he is, having decided that "*the badness of man was abundant in the earth and every inclination of the thoughts of his heart was only bad all the time,*" contemplating destroying every living thing on the face of the earth. (Gen. 6:5) Not only is all mankind issued with the death penalty, but every creature and their young roaming the earth or flying above it. They are viewed as collateral damage. Even creatures in the sea are doomed to perish in the roiling flood waters swamping the earth.

After the devastation of the flood, dead bodies are strewn about everywhere; the old and the young, men, women, little children, even infants not yet weaned, snatched away from their mothers' arms and drowned in the raging waters.

No doubt you have heard on the news accounts of countries where the death penalty is common, even for minor infringements of the law. But have you ever come across a modern day country where the death penalty has been extended to include the offspring of those convicted, including infants and children? Even the most backward and repressed of today's countries do not indulge in such indiscriminate violence.

The Bible tells us that only Noah and his family survived the biblical flood, together with the few animals that were sheltering in the ark, because he was considered righteous by God. He *"proved himself faultless among his contemporaries. Noah walked with the true God."* (Gen. 6:9). God's appraisal of Noah's character is accepted by almost all Christians, yet after the Flood, Noah became drunk with the wine produced from his vineyard and lay inebriated in his tent. On hearing that his grandson, Canaan had discovered him sprawled naked in this condition and had told his brothers, Noah cursed him with the words, *"Cursed be Canaan. Let him become the lowest slave to his brothers."* (Gen. 9:20-25) Noah's curse, with its far-reaching consequences, met with God's full approval.

Spoils of war

"And Jehovah went passing by before [Moses'] face and declaring, 'Jehovah, Jehovah, a God merciful and gracious, slow to anger and abundant in loving-kindness and truth.'"
Exodus 34:6

"Who is a God like you, one pardoning error and passing over transgression of the remnant of his inheritance? He will certainly not hold on to his anger forever, for he is delighting in loving-kindness." Micah 7:18

In light of these scriptures, we would expect that any person who has committed an offense but confessed to their crime before God, might receive forgiveness. In Joshua 7 we learn of an individual who did just that.

After the destruction of Jericho, Achan of the tribe of Judah disobeyed a decree that no spoils should be taken after the battle, and stole some items for himself. As a result, *"Jehovah's anger grew hot against the sons of Israel,"* (Joshua 7:1) and he turned his back on the Israelites. Eventually he revealed to Joshua who it was that had brought about this sorry state of affairs. Joshua then confronted Achan.

"Then Joshua said to Achan: 'My Son, render, please, glory to Jehovah the God of Israel and make confession to him, and tell me, please, What have you done? Do not hide it from me.' At this, Achan answered Joshua and said:

'For a fact I – I have sinned against Jehovah the God of Israel, and this way and that way I have done. When I got to see among the spoil an official garment from Shinar, a good-looking one, and two hundred shekels of silver and one gold bar, fifty shekels being its weight, then I wanted them

and I took them; and look! They are hidden in the earth in the midst of my tent with the money underneath it.'

"At once Joshua sent messengers, and they went running to the tent and look! It was hidden in his tent with the money underneath it. So they took them from the midst of the tent and brought them to Joshua and all the sons of Israel and poured them out before Jehovah." Joshua 7:19-23

Here we have a man who, when confronted with his crime, not only confessed, but revealed where he had hidden the stolen goods – surely, a good opportunity for the God of Israel to demonstrate his mercy and willingness to pardon error and pass over transgression.

"Joshua, and all Israel with him, now took Achan the son of Zerah and the silver and the official garment and the bar of gold and his sons and his daughters and his bull and his ass and his flock and his tent and everything that was his and they brought them up to the low plain of Achor. Then Joshua said: 'Why have you brought ostracism upon us? Jehovah will bring ostracism upon you on this day.'

"With that all Israel went pelting him with stones, after which they burned them with fire. Thus they stoned them with stones. And they proceeded to raise up over him a big pile of stones, down to this day. At this Jehovah turned away from his hot anger." Joshua verses 24-26

The Israelites' God had no intention of extending his divine forgiveness towards Achan. He had already instructed Joshua – before Achan had confessed to his crime – that Achan and all he possessed must be "burned with fire." (verse 15) Double standards? If you were to steal something, then later confess your crime, even revealing the location of the stolen goods, what punishment would you expect? Surely you would expect your confession to count in your favor. You would expect some allowance to be made for 'coming clean.' You would certainly not expect either yourself or your whole family, including your children and your pets, to answer for your crime with the death penalty.

To counter criticism of the violence espoused in the Old Testament, or Hebrew Scriptures, many Christian groups view the God of the New Testament as somehow different from that of the old Israelite God. They are at pains to distance themselves from the violent God of the Hebrew Scriptures, arguing that the Mosaic Law Covenant has been superseded by the peaceful teachings of Jesus Christ, as laid out in the New Testament.

In stark contrast, Jehovah's Witnesses specifically emphasize their connection with the God of the Hebrew Scriptures, elevating his name and declaring themselves to be his "Witnesses." They draw upon the connections between the God of the Israelites and the God of the early Christians, even inserting the name "Jehovah" into the Christian Greek text.

Nevertheless, let's examine the claim that the "new covenant" Jesus established is superior to the old Law Covenant. Can we be confident that the New Testament is a reliable guide that teaches love and tolerance and opposes violence?

New Testament and violence

During his ministry, Jesus did not offer any physical violence against individuals, bar one occasion when confronting money changers in the temple at Jerusalem. Jesus demonstrated his disapproval by targeting public property within temple grounds. No doubt the sight of a man overturning the tables, brandishing his whip and lashing out with it was enough to clear the area of buyers and sellers, fearful that physical violence might be directed towards them. (John 2:13-16; Mark 11.15-17; Mat. 21:12-13)

Apologists are anxious to ascribe his behavior on this occasion to "righteous indignation." Be that as it may, Jesus is not generally portrayed as a violent man. However, Jesus indicated that the divisive nature of his teachings, and his criticism of traditional Judaism would continue to result in conflict for his followers:

"Do not think I came to put peace upon the earth; I came to put, not peace, but a sword. For I came to cause division, with a man against his father, and a daughter against her mother, and a young wife against her mother-in-law. Indeed, a man's enemies will be persons of his own household. He that has greater affection for father or mother

than for me is not worthy of me; and he that has greater affection for son or daughter than for me is not worthy of me." Matthew 10:34-38.

Prescient though this pronouncement has proved to be, the knowledge that his own teachings would provoke such virulent division in the family household seems not to have caused him concern. Rather, he denounces those having greater affection for their families than for him.

"While he was yet speaking to the crowds, his mother and brothers took up a position outside seeking to speak to him. So someone said to him: 'Look! Your mother and your brothers are standing outside, seeking to speak to you.' As an answer he said to the one telling him: 'Who is my mother, and who are my brothers?' And extending his hand toward his disciples, he said: 'Look! My mother and my brothers! For whoever does the will of my Father who is in heaven, the same is my brother, and sister, and mother.'" Matthew 12:46-50

Even more chilling to contemplate is the fact that while the punishments and extirpations carried out by the God of Moses ended with the death of his victims, it is under the auspices of the "Prince of Peace" that we first learn of the grisly plan to resurrect the dead for further possible punishment and yet another round of executions, described as "the second death." (Revelation 21:8)

First of all, Jesus warns, "false prophets" will arise and mislead many people, but eventually, it will be necessary to sift out the good people from the bad. (Matthew 7:15)

"When the Son of Man arrives in all his glory, and all the angels with him, then he will sit down on his glorious throne. And all the nations will be gathered before him, and he will separate people one from another, just as a shepherd separates the sheep from the goats. And he will put the sheep on his right hand, but the goats on his left."

Note that for the "goats" the use of violence *en masse* is back. The "goats" are herded off *"into the everlasting fire prepared for the Devil and his angels."* (Matthew 25:31-46) A parallel prophecy indicates that on that day, the "goats" will greatly outnumber the sheep, because the road leading to life is described as narrow, with few entering through it into life, whereas *"Broad and spacious is the road leading to destruction, and many are the ones going in through it."*

It is worth stating that those who are designated "sheep" and those who are discarded as "goats" are largely determined by how they treat the person of Jesus Christ. In Matthew 11:20-24, for instance, Jesus denounces three towns because their inhabitants fail to respond to him, ending with the threat,

"I tell you that it will be more bearable for Sodom on the day of judgment than for you." (See also Matthew 23:35-38 and 26:24)

66

Notice also that the principle of whole towns, including women and children, collectively subjected to violent death, harks back to the story of the Benjamites in Judges 20 and 21.

Speaking again of his Second Coming, he warns,

"For just as the days of Noah were, so the presence of the Son of Man will be. For as they were in those days before the flood, eating and drinking, men marrying and women being given in marriage, until the day that Noah entered into the ark; and they took no note until the flood came and swept them all away, so the presence of the Son of Man will be."
Matthew 24:36-39

From this passage, it is abundantly clear that Jesus not only endorsed the mass execution of almost everybody on earth at the time of the Flood, but he fully expects to command a similar holocaust in the future, during his Second Coming. Assisting him will be the heavenly angels, who *"will go out and separate the wicked from among the righteous and will cast them into the fiery furnace. There is where [their] weeping and the gnashing of [their] teeth will be."* Matthew 13:49-50

He warns his own disciples, *"And do not become fearful of those who kill the body but cannot kill the soul; but rather be in fear of him that can destroy both soul and body in Gehenna."* Matthew 10:28

67

The injunction to be fearful of divine judgement is repeated in Luke 12 verse 5,

"But I will indicate to you whom to fear: Fear him who after killing has authority to throw into Gehenna. Yes, I tell you, fear this One."

Who are the ones likely to find themselves victims of Gehenna? First and foremost are those belonging to other religious persuasions (Matthew 3:7-13; 7:15-20), but fiery Gehenna is invoked for sins ranging from just looking at a woman "*so as to have a passion for her*" or becoming angry with a "brother," to money-changing and being on the wrong side of the fence when the angelic work of separating the 'sheep' from the 'goats' takes place. (Matthew 5:22, 28-29; 13:40-42; 23:33)

Other Christian writers

Paul explained the significance of Christ's Second Coming to the Thessalonians, reassuring them,

"...it is righteous on God's part to repay tribulation to those who make tribulation for you, but, to you who suffer tribulation, relief along with us at the revelation of the Lord Jesus from heaven with his powerful angels in a flaming fire, as he brings vengeance upon those who do not know God and those who do not obey the good news about our Lord Jesus. These very ones will undergo the judicial punishment of everlasting destruction from before the Lord and from the glory of his strength." 2 Thessalonians 1:7-9

There is no ambiguity about what kind of people will be on the receiving end of God's judgement. Those "*who do not know God and those who do not obey the good news about or Lord Jesus*" will suffer the death penalty.

> "*Do not be misled. Neither fornicators, nor idolaters, nor adulterers, nor men kept for unnatural purposes, nor men who lie with men, nor thieves, nor greedy persons, nor drunkards, nor revilers, nor extortioners will inherit God's Kingdom.*" 1 Corinthians 6:9,10

The book of Revelation adds,

> "*As for the cowards, and those without faith and those disgusting in their filth and the murderers and fornicators and those practicing spiritism and idolators and all the liars, their portion will be in the lake that burns with fire and sulphur. This means the second death.*" Revelation 21:8

A judicial punishment of everlasting destruction is pretty unequivocal, and the list of those in line for it is long. At the last trumpet, the dead finally will be resurrected, only to discover that many of their descendents are missing and that they themselves have risen to be judged as to whether or not they are eligible to receive the reward of everlasting life. Scrolls will be opened, and whoever is not found in the "*book of life*" will find themselves "*hurled into the lake of fire. This means the second death, the lake of fire.*" Revelation 20:11-15

I will have more to say later with respect to the violence portrayed in Bible prophecy, but I believe what we have considered here is sufficient to illustrate that, just as with the Hebrew Scriptures, the Christian Greek Scriptures are equally intent on violence, retribution, mass killing, and the imposition of the death penalty – with no exemptions for women, children, or infants. Believers are encouraged to harbor the conviction that those who reject their beliefs must be punished and put to death.

All the violence we have encountered in the Bible is read and accepted by fundamentalist Christians, Muslims, and Jews alike. Is it any wonder that, historically, many devotees of these religions have not only condoned acts of violence, but have committed them, claiming divine authority and sanction? If we take an objective, rather than a subjective, stance, we have to ask ourselves, can the wholesale murder of men, women, and children ever be justified? What about kidnap and rape? Is the invocation of a God sufficient to absolve the perpetrators of any wrongdoing? How then can those claiming to be moral read the above biblical accounts of atrocities and view them as holy texts? How do they reconcile the support they give to violent acts of murder and rapine with their belief in high moral standards?

Consider this. If the Bible is the word of God, surely we should expect it to contain the highest possible moral standards. Instead, wars, mass murder, ethnic cleansing, and rape take up a considerable portion of the books that make up the Hebrew Scriptures. Incidentally, Jehovah's 'rage' is mentioned over eighty times and his 'anger' well over two hundred times in the Hebrew scriptures alone.

As we have seen, Jesus read and endorsed the writings of the Hebrew prophets, and expected to take a leading role in the violence surrounding his Second Coming. In fact, the overarching theme of the New Testament is Christ's Second Coming and the "day of Jehovah," during which the entire inhabited earth will be judged as to whether or not they are worthy of everlasting life. (Acts 17:31)

Consequently, the main focus of Jehovah's Witnesses in their door-to-door preaching activity is to warn people of the imminence of the "day of Jehovah." They believe that those who turn them away will be judged by that action, marked as unrighteous, and will die at the hands of Jehovah at Armageddon. (Matthew 10:11-15; 2 Peter 3:3-7)

Reading matters

"Like eating, reading must be done selectively. Why eat food that offers no real nourishment or that may even poison you? In like manner, why read material, even casually, that can corrupt the mind and heart?" [12]

Having considered some of the violence displayed in the Bible, it is pertinent to ask what effect regular reading and study of these scriptures have on "the mind and heart" of believers.

71

All the atrocities that we have considered in the Old Testament, or Hebrew Scriptures, took place for one reason only. The scriptures themselves tell us that it was because the Israelites believed themselves to be the "chosen" people of Yahweh, or Jehovah, to be his *special property out of all the peoples that are on the surface of the ground.*" (Deut. 7:6) The Israelites claimed that God told them to clear all other peoples off the land of Palestine, so that they could occupy it for themselves, giving his divine sanction for them to commit whatever genocide was necessary in order to bring that about.

Similarly, in the New Testament, or Christian Greek Scriptures, Jesus' disciples expect those who do not belong to their Christian organization to be swept away in a tide of violence on the Day of Jehovah.

Tribalism

Tribal societies still exist in remote places like Papua New Guinea, the Andaman Islands, and the Amazon, living in a prehistoric manner, either deliberately isolated from modern civilization, or having only minimal contact. Study of these tribes gives us valuable insight into how ancient peoples probably lived in Europe and the Middle East.

The tendency to view other tribes as sub-human ensures that warfare is a constant feature of tribal lives, with a significant proportion of tribal peoples killed in violent

72

ways. Jared Diamond has spent much of his career living among the remote tribes of Papua New Guinea, and has recently published a book of his observations.[13] When living with a mountain tribe, Diamond was warned by them to keep away from the neighboring River People, who are viewed by Mountain People as dangerous sub-humans, or demonised devils. Any Mountain People entering River People's territory are killed immediately, and vice versa. Their violence, however, is only directed at the other tribes. Within each tribe, individuals are loving and altruistic and are willing to give their lives for each other.

From studies like those of Diamond, tribal behavior is recognized as being deeply rooted in all modern humans. In particular, many religions are inherently tribal. Since most religions have very ancient roots, they have fossilized the tribal beliefs and moral values of the societies that created them. Like tribal peoples, members of fundamentalist religious groups are generally loving and kind to each other, yet most of them subscribe to the view that they alone are God's chosen people, and they are inclined to paint members of other religions as somehow inferior and less worthy. A program of misinformation about people outside their religion is used to bolster such prejudices.

In contrast, the secular world has long come to recognize that vilification of other races, national groups, or religious persuasions has the effect of elevating one class of people over another. It encourages exclusivity and tribalism; it fosters an uncaring, superior attitude, and provides the perfect breeding ground for discrimination of the worst kind. The blacker others are painted, the better individuals feel about themselves. It is a base form of self-aggrandizement and conceit, in which others become convenient scapegoats and are blamed for all ills. They can be treated in despicable ways, while the perpetrators exempt themselves from guilt. Particularly in the case of the worship of a deity, a god or gods can be invoked, giving divine sanction for the mistreatment and brutality heaped upon those considered inferior. Such absolution deadens the conscience and renders those meting out "justice" impervious to feelings of empathy or remorse.

Holy writings and human behavior

Such was the case in medieval Christendom. Instead of separating themselves from the secular culture of cruelty in dealing out punishment to those judged guilty of offense, sadistic torture was sanctioned by the Church with the personal authorization of Pope Innocent IV in 1251. Those accused of heresy, blasphemy, or apostasy were systematically tortured by Dominican monks in order to extract "confessions" in the belief that it would save the immortal souls of their victims from eternal damnation. Shocking though their cruelty appears to present-day sensibilities, the fact is that the scriptures encouraged them in their discrimination and

74

condemnation of those who did not hold identical beliefs to the established Church.

Jesus himself said, *"If anyone does not remain in union with me, he is cast out as a branch and is dried up; and men gather those branches up and pitch them into the fire and they are burned."* John 15:5

This scripture was taken literally, and was the justification for those considered heretics to be strangled and burned at the stake.

Crusades

Consider the bloody history of the Crusades, a saga familiar to most people, but what really motivated ordinary individuals and armies of men to undertake an arduous journey halfway around the world to fight in defense of a city they had never seen? Why would they undergo such hardship, with the prospect of perhaps never returning home?

The answer is that they were inspired and encouraged by members of the established Church to take up arms against the Muslims. It was a "Holy War," in which the holy city of Jerusalem had to be defended against God-defying barbarians. Preachers read out scriptures describing the Israelite battles for the "holy land," and advocated slaughter from the pulpit. In 1188, Baldwin, the

Archbishop of Canterbury, together with his companion, Gerald, Archdeacon of Brecon, set out on a six-week missionary journey through Wales to further the cause of the Third Crusade, which was to recapture Jerusalem from Saladin.[14] Their campaign proved successful, as Gerald records,

"After the sermon which was given in Hay [on Wye], we saw a great number of men who wanted to take the Cross come running towards the castle where the Archbishop was, leaving their cloaks behind in the hands of the wives and friends who had tried to hold them back." [15]

The Archbishop persuaded the people flocking to hear his sermons that they would not incur bloodguilt, or guilt resulting from bloodshed, if they slew Muslims because God would absolve them of their sins. In fact, engaging in battle was viewed as honorable. Gerald speaks highly of a blind man who mounted a warhorse and charged forward in the front line of battle, "but was immediately struck down by a blow from a sword and so ended his life with honour." [16]

The New World

The idea of "a people for special possession" also comes to the fore in the grab for land in North America. With the discovery of the New World, Europeans began to encounter "primitive" peoples they had never imagined to exist. How did they view these Native Americans, and how were they treated? In *Conquistadors*, Michael Wood describes the general reaction of new arrivals.

"To some, the Native Americans were untouched by the word of God and had been debased by the Devil; to others, they were a remnant from before the Fall, living in an innocence long lost by the corrupted West. Either way it was almost impossible, throughout this whole period, for the indigenous peoples to be considered humans in their own right. The Europeans brought with them the baggage of centuries of Eurocentrism, and Christian monotheism, which espoused one truth, one time and one version of reality."..."Europeans endlessly debated whether or not they had souls. Or were they people like them? ...Was their religion the direct work of the Devil? Such arguments spawned a host of pronouncements: laws for Indians, rituals of submission, utopian texts, sermons, lectures, [and] papal bulls." [17]

The native North American Indians were considered no barrier to progress by Christian settlers clutching their Bibles, who arrived in the New World by ship from other countries. They had no interest or respect for American Indian culture and tradition within the diverse tribes of peoples inhabiting the land. Instead, the native inhabitants were uniformly bundled together under the pejorative label, "primitive savages," and considered a scourge to be cleared off the land so that the settlers could occupy it for themselves.

77

A photograph of the last four "full-blooded" Tasmanian Aborigines C.1860s. Truganini, the last to survive, is seated at far right.

How is such inhumane treatment possible? Because Christians of past centuries, fed on a diet of Bible scriptures, believed they were the ones exclusively favored by God, and therefore inherently superior to people belonging to "inferior" racial groups and/or alternative belief systems.

Still in the nineteenth century, the British treatment of Tasmanians followed the same depressing pattern, fueled by the same Biblical ideal. The mainland Aborigines and those on Van Diemen's Land (Tasmania) were considered an inferior race; primitive; incapable of human emotions, thoughts, and feelings. The British felt they had a perfect right to push them aside and occupy the land.[18] Today, there are no full-blooded Aboriginal Tasmanians left in existence.

European expansion and appropriation of territory continued to be justified on the grounds that there was an ineluctable mission to introduce Christianity to the godless people already occupying the land. The perpetrators of atrocities held the unshakeable belief that they had both the divine right (bolstered by more than one Roman Catholic Papal bull to that effect), and racial superiority necessary to civilize the rest of the world.

Moving on to modern times, sectarian violence fueled by belief in the Bible was at the heart of the conflict in Northern Ireland, a bitter civil war between Catholics and Protestants, each side believing themselves to be the ones favored by God. The conflict has religious roots stretching back centuries into the past, and over time has been responsible for the death of thousands of Northern Ireland's citizens.

More recently, the horrific events that unfolded on 11 September 2001 in New York exemplify the dreadful reality of irrational belief in divine favor. Extremist Muslims sacrificed their own lives and those of thousands of others, motivated by a desire to please their God and to strike a blow against "unbelievers." Ironically, the Q'uran contains many references to people and events found in the Bible. Since the Q'uran is believed to supersede the

Bible, stories in the Bible that are compatible with it are accepted, and therefore known to Muslims.

Exactly the same belief and motivation can be observed today in the form of the Palestine-Israeli conflict. The continuation of this conflict is supported by the same scriptures we have just considered. The Israelis still believe that God gave the land of Palestine to the Israelites and that they have a God-given right to occupy it. The ongoing illegal settlement of Palestinian lands in contravention of a UN resolution is tolerated because it is supported by active fundamentalist Christians in the United States who have read these same biblical scriptures. As the US has a United Nations veto, peace remains elusive. It is a sad indictment of these ancient texts that they are responsible for the ongoing violence and death of innocent people in our own time.

Just as Jewish people in the twentieth century began to claim Palestine as their rightful new homeland, so Jehovah's Witnesses believe that the original Jewish settlement of Palestine prefigures what they, as "Jews on the inside," can expect Jehovah, to provide for them by right. (Romans 2:28,29; 3:29) The only difference is that Jehovah's Witnesses expect to take possession, not only of Palestine, but of the entire planet as their homeland, reserved for their own exclusive use after the violent "day of Jehovah." (2 Peter 3:12)

80

After examining in some detail the Bible's attitude to morality and violence, it is pertinent to ask, where did the Bible come from? Can it really be the word of God?

BIBLE CANON

Eithne felt weary with the constant heat, dust, and discomfort of travel. She had known from the start that her pilgrimage to the shrine of Hagia Thekla would be a difficult venture, but had she known of all the troubles she would encounter along the way, perhaps she would never have come. Perhaps, without the constant attendance and solicitous ministrations of her dear son Aelius, she would never have accomplished it. But here she was, within sight of her goal. All she needed to do was to keep placing one foot in front of the other. One foot... and then the other...

She paused for breath, her hands resting on her narrow hips. Below her, the *Mare Nostrum*, translucent turquoise, stretched as far as the eye could see. On its shores lay the city of Seleucia, white and gleaming in the glare of the sun sliding down the vault of the sky. Soon the walls of the city would turn a mellow gold and the sea would deepen to indigo.

Above her head, Eithne could see what her eyes had longed to rest upon all these years. The complex of Hagia Thekla perched atop its ancient hill. She had heard descriptions of it many times. She knew that no less than three basilicas had been built there together with a large public bath and a number of cisterns, all the better to accommodate the constant stream of pilgrims visiting

Thekla's shrine.   Nothing had prepared her for the experience, however.   The sheer breath-taking sight of it perched so high above the city, like New Jerusalem, shimmering in the heat rising from the parched ground.

She had been informed by returning pilgrims that Thekla's shrine was in a cave at the southern end of the hill overlooking the city. There, a small, three-aisled basilica had been built into a natural grotto of limestone. Well, she would take her place in the stream of pilgrims entering within, then spend the night here on this hilltop in order to pray and read through the whole Acts of Thekla. She would give heartfelt thanks to God for his graciousness in allowing her to fulfill her most cherished dream, despite her unworthiness.

Aelius gave her a quick, sideways glance. "You know the *Acts of Paul and Thekla* is a forgery, the work of a common presbyter, don't you?"

Eithne gave a snort of derision.   "I have heard this rumor, yes, but I choose to ignore it. Why do you speak of it now?"

"It's not a rumor, it- it's the truth."   Aelius turned to her in earnest. "Why do you ignore it, my mother? What is the use of worshiping at the shrine of someone who does not even exist?"

Eithne stared at him, exasperated. At twenty-four, he was a full-grown man, and yet he still retained the air of someone a lot younger. Why was he suddenly difficult now, when they were within sight of their destination?

"Who says Thekla does not exist, when devout Christians have been visiting her shrines for centuries? Who?" she demanded. "Naturally there are always skeptics and unbelievers who will say our holy writings are forgeries. Must we listen to all of them? Pah! We would have nothing left."

Aelius looked uncomfortable, but continued, "Tertullian speaks of the confessions of the very man who wrote the Acts. He himself condemned the worship of Thekla."

"It is not worship, Aelius, my son. And who is this man, this presbyter, to say that what he wrote was not inspired by the Almighty God? I should say he is a man lacking in faith; that is all."

Aelius frowned and was silent, gazing out towards the far horizon where dabs of faded calico indicated the presence of ships plying their trade between Asia Minor and Antioch.

"Did not Thekla appear to Emperor Zeno of Rome in a dream, to inform him that soon he would be restored to office?" Eithne persisted. "And did it not happen just as she prophesied? Zeno himself built a magnificent church in her honor in the city out of gratitude for her intercession on his behalf. Did we not visit that church this very day? What more proof do you need?"

Aelius shook his head, a note of belligerence creeping into his voice.

"I think perhaps she exists only in the minds of all those foolish enough to continue flocking to her shrines. I –"

"Enough! You should be ashamed of yourself, Aelius! I don't know what's come over you! If you feel so strongly about it, you need not accompany me any further. I will continue on alone."

Eithne felt suddenly furious. She pulled her woven shawl more tightly around her shoulders and marched on, conscious that Aelius held all her possessions for their overnight stay in a capacious bag strapped to his back. She forced herself to keep struggling upwards, her leather sandals sliding over the loose white stones, sending them rattling back down the slope. After a moment, to her relief, Aelius drew up close behind her.

"I did not mean to upset you, mother," he sighed. "I'm sorry. But what do you hope to gain? What can Thekla do for you that the Lord Jesus Christ cannot? Is he not your redeemer? Is he not the one who may intercede with God on your behalf?"

At last Eithne was given the key to what this was all about. Aelius had been talking to a group of Christians in Seleucia earlier in the day. No doubt they were of another persuasion, one that did not approve of Thekla, swayed instead by the bitter invective of Tertullian against the descendants of Eve:

"Do you not realise that Eve is you? The curse God pronounced on your sex weighs still on the world... You are the devil's gateway, you desecrated the fatal tree, you first betrayed

the law of God, you who softened up with your cajoling words the man against whom the devil could not prevail by force..." [19]

She took a deep breath.

"You misunderstand me, my son. Of course Thekla believed Jesus was our *'salvation and a foundation of life immortal and whoever does not believe in him will not live but will die forever.'* [20] Are her words not true?"

Aelius nodded in grudging consent.

Eithne pressed home her advantage. "And it is also true that Jesus was the first of all those resurrected to sit at the right hand of God. All the apostles have taken their places beside him including the lady Thekla, a fellow slave who accompanied the Apostle Paul on so many of his missionary journeys. She herself said, *'If you desire riches, the Lord will give them to you through me.'"* [21]

She touched Aelius lightly on the arm.

"Know that in my heart Thekla exists, a real woman who hears and understands my prayers. I know she speaks for me before the Almighty. Do you understand this?"

Aelius frowned for a moment, and she feared he was lost to her. Then that sweet smile she loved so well spread across his face.

"You are truly devout, my mother," he told her, placing his arm around her shoulders. "Come, we will enter her shrine together."

***

Early Christianity and the making of the Bible

Saint Thekla
Source: eikonografos.com

Jehovah's Witnesses are convinced that they share exactly the same beliefs as the early Christians and possess the very same scriptures with which they were familiar. The truth of the matter is that the early Christians did not have an agreed collection of holy writings with which to verify points of theocratic debate, apart from the Hebrew Scriptures.

Although most of the books and letters that were eventually collected into the New Testament had been written by the second century, they had not yet been gathered together into a widely recognized and authoritative canon of scripture. For this reason, it is not possible to get back to a pure, single narrative, first-century Christianity because such a Christianity never existed. Early Christians were not highly organized from the start, with a coherent set of beliefs that they were immediately able to disseminate throughout the known world under the direction of a unified Governing Body.

87

The Bible book of Acts of the Apostles describes some of the uncertainties that abounded in those years after Jesus' death. When Paul became a Christian, around AD 37-40, he began to assert his own authority and influence over the Christian movement. Considering himself a rival to the apostles who had been companions of Jesus throughout his ministry, Paul chose never to refer to Jesus' life on earth, but concentrated instead on the significance of the resurrected Christ. However, there was constant controversy. Paul was of the opinion that Gentile converts wanting to become Christians should not need to become Jews first, but his opinion on the matter was by no means widely accepted by all followers of Jesus. Acts chapter 15 indicates that there were dissenting voices and groups taking an opposing line. In *Lost Christianities,* Professor of Religious Studies, Bart D. Ehrman, a leading authority on early Christianity, expresses it this way:

"Even more striking, Paul's own letters indicate that there were outspoken, sincere, and active Christian leaders who vehemently disagreed with him on this score and considered Paul's views to be a corruption of the true message of Christ." [22]

The controversy was not solved during Paul's lifetime, but continued to rage for centuries.

At the same time as letters from Paul were circulating amongst the newly established congregations, apprising them of his views on the controversy, other books and letters began to circulate that were equally impressive, claiming to have been written by Jesus' apostles. Many of these other books and letters coming into circulation were initially accepted as sacred and inspired by early Christians, and they were revered just as much as the New Testament books that grace the pages of the Bible as we know it today.

There were letters purporting to have been written by Paul himself. They do not appear in the Bible, but we know they existed because Paul's second letter to the Thessalonians warns the congregation to beware of false letters claiming to be from him. There was originally more than one book of Acts. The *Acts of Paul and Thecla* (or Thekla) contains the history of a female convert and associate of Paul.[23] She eventually became a cult hero, with devotees flocking to her shrines, including the pilgrim Egeria, who wrote an account of her journey in AD 384, of which only a fragment survives. Thecla was revered for centuries, almost as much as Mary, the Mother of God, despite the condemnation of Tertullian, a prominent early Christian authority who exposed the work as a forgery.

"Among several pseudoepigraphical works attributed to Paul, including 1 and 2 Timothy and Titus (The Pastoral Epistles) and 2 Corinthians, *the Acts of Paul and Thecla* was known to be a forgery at the time. Tertullian makes the contention in his treatise *On Baptism*, no doubt to refute any justification that it offered for women to preach and baptize.

89

"But if certain Acts of Paul, which are falsely so named, claim the example of Thecla for allowing women to teach and to baptize, let men know that in Asia the presbyter who compiled that document, thinking to add of his own to Paul's reputation, was found out, and though he professed he had done it for love of Paul, was deposed from his position. How could we believe that Paul should give a female power to teach and to baptize, when he did not allow a woman even to earn by her own right? Let them keep silence, he says, and ask their husbands at home." [24]

Once, there existed a gospel claiming to be written by Jesus' closest disciple, Simon Peter, and other gospels by Mary Magdalene, James, Nicodemus, and Philip. There was an Acts of Thomas, written by Jesus' brother, Didymus Judas Thomas; an Acts of John, Acts of Paul, Acts of Peter, and even an Acts of Pilate, exonerating him for his involvement in Jesus' death. There was an Epistle of Barnabas, an Epistle of Clement, an Epistle of Ignatius, and many more. Other writings include apocalyptic visions and treatises such as *The Secret Book of John*, *Origin of the World,* and *Shepherd of Hermas.* The Revelation according to John was not alone. There was also an Apocalypse of Paul, and more than one Apocalypse of Peter. All of these titles were eventually set aside as works not written under inspiration. Why? Why did nearly all of Paul's letters continue to be considered inspired, and yet none of these other writings? Why does the New Testament consist almost entirely of Paul's letters?

True, some of these alternative gospels later proved to be written by persons other than the apostles whom they claimed to be, no doubt with the intention of borrowing authority to express views and opinions of their own, or to support one side of an argument or dispute between rival religious communities. Whatever the intentions, all these writings exerted a powerful influence, resulting in diverse beliefs and practices amongst various early Christian groups.

Influential figures in the early Christian community interpreted these writings in different ways, each gathering its group of ardent Christian advocates. Among these groups were the Marcionites and the Ebionites, the former being by far the most successful. Marcionites were followers of the second-century theologian, Marcion (nee c.AD 100). They eliminated everything Jewish from their worship, even the Jewish scriptures and their Jewish God. They were heavily influenced by the letters of Paul, concerning the difference between the Law of the Jews and the superior teachings of Christ, which did away with salvation through adherence to the Mosaic Law Covenant. This made it attractive to potential pagan converts with the result that new churches sprang up wherever Marcion set foot during his missionary journeys. These churches thrived for centuries, to the extent that in some parts of Asia Minor they offered the first accepted form of Christianity, and comprised of the most devotees claiming to be Christian.

In direct contrast, the lesser known Ebionites were Jews who believed that Jewish practice was fundamental to gaining God's approval. The Christian God was the God of the Jews. As for the teachings of Paul – that faith apart from works of Law was acceptable to God – they viewed these as heretical, and therefore rejected Paul's letters. Certainly the Ebionites' form of Christianity leant heavily on the book of Matthew, which concentrates on the importance of Jewishness for followers of Christ.

Montanists (including Tertullian, whom we met earlier), were followers of Montanus, a Phrygian in what is now west central Turkey, who believed himself to be a prophet receiving divine revelations directly from God. For Montanists, such revelations took precedence over the known scriptures. Montanists were ethically strict, believing that the end of the world was near, and that people needed to be warned in order to prepare for it. God would very soon judge the inhabited earth, and then the kingdom of God would arrive, ushering in the reign of Jesus Christ. Montanist Christians believed they must devote their lives to the coming kingdom and be willing to defend their faith to the point of death.

Naturally, each of these groups claimed a pedigree linking them back directly to the apostles and to Jesus himself. Inevitably, the authority of many of the sacred writings, espoused to support their respective stances, was hotly disputed. It should come as no surprise, then, that the collection of twenty-seven books now accepted as sacred and inspired are those chosen by the winners of these conflicts. The prominence of the Apostle Paul's thirteen letters and his role in the establishment of Christianity at that time can now be understood as a product of that selective choice. Christian letters that disagreed with Paul's teachings were reviled and discarded. Many of them have been irretrievably lost.

Bart Ehrman describes the situation:

"Virtually all forms of modern Christianity, whether they acknowledge it or not, go back to one form of Christianity that emerged as victorious from the conflicts of the second and third centuries. This one form of Christianity decided what was 'correct' Christian perspective; it decided who could exercise authority over Christian belief and practice; and it determined what forms of Christianity would be marginalized, set aside, destroyed. It also decided which books to canonize into Scripture and which books to set aside as 'heretical,' teaching false ideas." (*Lost Christianities,* p.4)

As Ehrman goes on to note, the victors obscured the facts and rewrote the history of these conflicts, making it appear that their view had always been the most prevalent, and that other opposing views, their adherents and their supporting scriptures were merely the erroneous and misguided beliefs of fringe, heretical elements.

Which form of Christianity eventually won the day?

In AD 312 the Roman Emperor Constantine, having won a major battle at Milvian Bridge outside Rome, declared his undying gratitude to "the supreme deity," which Christians understood to mean the God of the Christians. Many historians are skeptical of his commitment to Christian mores, some maintaining that Constantine's main concern was more likely to have been to ensure that growing Christian communities supported his imperial rule. How could this be done?

Marble head of Constantine the Great, Emperor of the Roman Empire, and a convert to Christianity. Roman, 4th Century.

At the time of Constantine's succession in York, the Roman Empire was unstable and divided into sections governed by four different Caesars. Constantine ruled only part of the empire, but he wanted to reunite it and breathe new life into it. He observed that Christians operated within a fully functioning hierarchy – a state within a state – separate from Roman society, and that the bishops commanded complete and effective control over their flock. How could he use this to his advantage?

He determined to use the bishops and the internal structure of their Christianity for his own ends. He appointed them as judges to administer the law. They were given money, power, and authority to act, as long as they ensured that their flock remained subservient to the empire.

However, Constantine was still threatened by the endemic political and doctrinal disunity of the Christian Greeks. Historian, Charles Freeman comments:

"What is usually concealed in the histories of early Christianity is the tensions between different groups. This is partly because the earliest history of the church, Eusebius' fourth-century *Ecclesiastic History*, which was accepted as an authoritative account for centuries to come, glossed over these, presenting instead a church united in doctrine, hallowed by the blood of its martyrs and ready to take its rightful place in society with the ending of persecution. Yet in his *Life of Constantine...* Eusebius is forced to accept that there was often violent discord between Christian communities, particularly over rival interpretations of doctrine. This discord was only to be intensified as the [Roman] emperors tried to integrate Christianity into the state." [25]

At the Council of Nicaea in AD 325, the first Ecumenical Council of the Christian Church took place, calling upon its bishops from all over the known world to gather together in order to establish consensus on major points of faith and practice. The council dealt not with local schisms, but with fundamental issues of doctrine; most significantly, the relationship between God the Father and the Son of God. The bishops decided on the main theological positions that had emerged out of past conflicts, which meant that writings in support of those positions were favored as holy and authentic, and the others rejected.

Heated debates continued nonetheless, and it was not until AD 367 that the Christian theologian, Athanasius of Alexandria (an attendee at the Council of Nicaea), drew up a definitive list of books to be included in the Bible canon that matches our list today. His list corresponded well enough with what the majority of orthodox Christians of the day were willing to accept, and so it prevailed. It was later championed by Augustine of Hippo at the Synod of Hippo in AD 393. The text of the proceedings is not available to historians, but those of the Third Synod of Carthage, four years later, summarized the earlier proceedings:

> "The canonical Scriptures are these... Of the New Testament: the Gospels, four books; the Acts of the Apostles, one book; the Epistles of Paul, thirteen; of the same to the Hebrews, one Epistle; of Peter, two; of John, apostle, three; of James, one; of Jude, one; the Revelation of John. Concerning the confirmation of this canon, the church across the sea shall be consulted." [26]

Theological debates in later centuries can be understood as further refinements built upon already established outcomes of the disputes of earlier centuries. For most forms of Christianity within the orthodox tradition, Roman Catholicism, Eastern Orthodoxy, and Protestantism, the matter of canonicity was more or less solved. Although a few adjustments to the canonical list were made by some parts of the Christian church, all other writings considered "uninspired" at that time were soon viewed as heretical and were banned, buried, lost, or destroyed.

Bible readers today are often unaware of the conflicts surrounding the Bible canon and that the beliefs they hold now are largely a product of the outcome of the political maneuvering and debates of bishops of previous centuries.

The power and control exercised by the established Church over the centuries was immense. During the period known as the Dark Ages, medical progress stagnated, universities closed, and literature, plays, theatre, and music were stifled or banned outright. Education and careers were restricted and channeled through the Church. By AD 412, when Cyril became Archbishop of Alexandria, religious intolerance had grown to monstrous proportions and punishments for non-compliance were severe. Cyril used his attendants, or *parabalani*, to assert his authority and fill the city with terror. The Roman city prefect, Orestes was attacked and injured by a mob of monks, and *parabalani* are believed to have also been involved in the most shocking and gruesome murder of Hypatia, a respected Alexandrian philosopher and mathematician. She was murdered in the street by a Christian mob and her body torn apart.

Christianity had become rigid and fossilized, but still it continued to exercise control over millions of people over the thousand years from Constantine to the Reformation. To this day, the form of Christianity hammered out by the warring bishops in the Roman Empire has continued largely unchanged. Those who accept the Bible as it stands are accepting the judgement of early bishops. For this reason, they must also accept that the edited version of Christianity contained within its pages would not necessarily be recognizable to an early Christian.

Are the books contained in the Bible canon reliably authentic?

In recent decades, many scholars have been re-examining Bible texts in order to re-establish whether or not they are authentic. Professor of Religious Studies and Judaic Studies, Ross S. Kraemar, speaking of early Judaism and early Christianity, acknowledges the fact that,

> "...a significant portion of the texts that have come down to us are either anonymous – without any ascription of authorship – or pseudonymous – attributed to someone unlikely if not impossible to be the author. In a few cases, the author's name may be known, but virtually nothing else. Most of the New Testament, except for the undisputed letters of Paul, falls into these categories, as does virtually everything else in Jewish apocrypha and pseudepigrapha." [27]

Ehrman is also convinced that many pseudonymous writings appear in the Bible.

> "If, then, by 'apostolic' book we mean, 'book actually written by an apostle,' most of the books that came to be included in the New Testament are not apostolic." [28]

His current list of false epistles includes Ephesians, Colossians, 2 Thessalonians, 1 Timothy, 2 Timothy, Titus, James, 1 Peter (still debated), 2 Peter, and Jude.

Another scholar, P.H. Wicksteed, has reached similar conclusions.

> "The two letters to Timothy and the letter to Titus were certainly composed long after the death of Paul... It is more than possible that the letters to the Ephesians and Colossians are also unauthentic, and the same suspicion rests, perhaps, on the first, but certainly on the second of the Epistles to the Thessalonians" [29]

What about the four Gospels? Can we at least rely upon them as eyewitness accounts of Jesus' ministry? In fact, all four books were written anonymously over forty years after Jesus' death. It is thought that these books were compiled from a selection of anecdotes or word-of-mouth accounts of Jesus' life and teachings, passed on from person to person after his death. None of them are penned in the first person, as eye-witness accounts would be, nor do any of them make this claim. Not until a century after they were written were they attributed to Matthew, Mark, Luke, and John. Why so late in the day?

Ehrman believes it may be because during the second century proto-orthodox Christians recognized a need for apostolic authorities, so they attributed these books to apostles (Matthew and John) and close companions of apostles (Mark and Luke), commenting,

> "Most scholars today have abandoned these identifications, and recognize that the books were written by otherwise unknown but relatively well-educated Greek-speaking (and writing) Christians during the second half of the first century." [30] (Lost Christianities, p.234-235)

Finally,

> *"A revelation by Jesus Christ, which God gave him, to show his slaves the things that must shortly take place. And he sent forth his angel and presented [it] in signs through him to his slave John."* Revelation 1:1

The book of Revelation was written by the Apostle John while in exile on the island of Patmos – or so it has been believed for centuries. True, the book was written by someone called John, but nowhere does he claim to be John, the son of Zebedee, one of the twelve apostles. This was a cause for such controversy that the churches of Syria, Palestine, and Cappadocia, Central Anatolia, did not include the book of Revelation in their Bible canon until the fifth century AD.[31]   Ehrman writes,

> "The Revelation (or Apocalypse) of John was widely rejected by proto-orthodox Christians in the eastern part of the empire during the first four centuries, who argued that it was not written by the apostle." [32]

Apostasy

Jehovah's Witnesses believe that by the end of the first century a 'Great Apostasy' took place, a falling away from the true teachings of Christ, and a corruption of the Christian congregation. (2 Thessalonians 2:3; Matthew 7:15; Matthew 13:24-30; and Matthew 13:36-43) Accordingly, they believe that Christendom is entirely apostate, and is described in the Bible as part of "*Babylon the Great, the mother of the harlots and of the disgusting things of the earth.*" As such, they anticipate its destruction by God before the outbreak of Armageddon. (Revelation 17) Yet, at the same time, Jehovah's Witnesses are prepared to accept the idea that during this 'Great Apostasy', God inspired Christendom's bishops to undertake an accurate assessment of all the various competing books available for inclusion in the Bible canon, and make the correct choices. The resultant compilation finally agreed upon by these 'apostate' bishops is accepted by Jehovah's Witnesses as the infallible word of God.

LAST DAYS

The promise

Imagine for a moment that you are living in the time of Jesus. You have heard many amazing stories circulating about him, and you are curious to find out what it is all about. Now you learn that this charismatic young man is touring the villages of Caesarea Philippi, north of the Sea of Galilee, gathering crowds of people to hear his words. Eager to see him, you travel perhaps many miles and now, at last, you find yourself in an excited crowd of people, jostling your way forward, listening intently to hear what the Master has to say.

"If anyone desires to come after me," he begins, "let him deny himself, take up his cross, and follow me." [33]

Gradually, you nudge your way forwards, listening to his voice, hanging onto his every word until, at last, you have a clear view of the man himself. Now imagine the tingling sensation running up and down your spine as he delivers the following, thrilling promise.

"Truly I say to you, There are some of those standing here that will not taste death at all until first they see the kingdom of God already come in power." (Mark 8:34-9:1)

Is there any possibility that you would have thought to yourself, "Ah yes, these words do not apply to me. They are obviously meant for people living thousands of years in the future"?

Jehovah's Witnesses believe exactly that.

To anyone reading Jesus' words without bias, such a conclusion must seem illogical. It is only too obvious to an objective observer that Jesus was speaking to the audience *standing right there in front of him*. Jesus' disciples followed him because they believed his promises would make a difference to their lives. Why else would his disciples rally to his command to leave their lucrative fishing businesses and abandon their wives, their children, and their homes in order to follow him? (Matthew 4:19,20; Mark 1:18-20; Luke 5:11) If these men did not believe the kingdom was imminent, their astonishingly cavalier behavior towards their families would have constituted an irresponsible and immoral act. In fact, if Jesus issued that command in full knowledge that his prophecy did not apply to them, he could be seen as self-serving and callous.

Why then, are Jehovah's Witnesses so keen to ascribe Jesus' words to a time far in the future, to the time period we are living in now? A time period they believe to be "the last days?" (2 Peter 3:3; 2 Timothy 3:1) A compelling reason for an alternative interpretation is, of course, that those listening to Jesus' words died without seeing the fulfillment of the promise. In other words, the prophecy failed.

In his first letter to the Thessalonians, the Apostle Paul is convinced that Jesus' return is still imminent and that it will take place within his lifetime.

> *"For this is what we tell you by Jehovah's word, that **we the living who survive to the presence of the Lord** shall in no way precede those who have fallen asleep [in death]; because the Lord himself will descend from heaven with a commanding call, with an archangel's voice and with God's trumpet, and those who are dead in union with Christ will rise first. Afterward **we the living who are surviving** will, together with them, be caught away in clouds to meet the Lord in the air; and thus we shall always be with [the] Lord."* 1 Thess. 4:15-17 *[Emphasis mine]*

Paul's description makes it clear that he expects Jesus' Second Coming to come suddenly, unexpectedly, but soon. Again, history demonstrates that his expectations were false.

The Last Days in modern times

Today, Jehovah's Witnesses believe that since 1914 we have been living in the "last days." Soon, Christ will lead his heavenly armies into battle on "the day of Jehovah against all the nations" at Armageddon. (Obadiah 15; Revelation 16:16 KJV) What convinces them that it is close at hand?

104

In a parallel prophecy in the twenty-fourth chapter of Matthew, Jesus' disciples asked him, *"What sign will signal your return and the end of the world?"* (verse 3, New Living Translation) In answer, Jesus described a number of specific world events that would alert those on the watch to his imminent return in power and glory (Matthew 24:3-25:31; see chapter heading, '1914'). Significantly, he paused along the way to reassure his disciples with these words:

"Truly I say to you that this generation will by no means pass away until all these things occur." Matthew 24:34

Again, at first reading, this prophecy appears to be referring to the near future, to a time close to the people contemporary with Jesus. His listeners appear to be *"this generation"* who will not pass away until all the signs have taken place and *"the end of the world"* or *"the end of the system of things"* comes.

To modern-day readers who believe implicitly in the absolute authenticity of the Bible, it is unacceptable for Jesus' prophecies to have failed, so they reason that this passage and the parallel prophecy at Mark 9:1 must be referring to a generation yet future. Jehovah's Witnesses believe that *"this generation"* referred to a small but privileged class of people they refer to as "anointed ones," (2 Corinthians 1:21) who would see all the signs pointing to Jesus' return in all his glory as King, and would recognize them. According to all their calculations, the "*last days*" and the final end would occur in the year 1914.

The generation that saw the signs Jesus spoke of taking place in 1914 – and were old enough to recognize them – would not "*pass away*," but would be raised up instantly into God's kingdom, established in heaven in that same year. There, they would rule as kings with Christ for a thousand years over an earth wiped clean of wicked people. (Revelation 14:1-3; 20:4; 21:1-4, 8) Clearly, this didn't happen. 1914 came and went without any of the "anointed" class being snatched up into the heavens. The First World War failed to culminate in Armageddon, and the wicked were not destroyed by God in a global holocaust.

In the first valid attempt to explain how people deal with discredited doomsday predictions, Leon Festinger (et al) put forward his classic theory of cognitive dissonance, published in 1956.

Festinger's theory can account for the psychological consequences of failed expectations. It proposes, first of all, that there are five preconditions under which to expect increased fervor following the disconfirmation of belief.

- A belief must be held with deep conviction and it must have some relevance to action, that is, to what
- the believer does or how he behaves.

- The person holding the belief must be committed to it; that is, for the sake of his belief, he must have taken some important action that is difficult to undo. In general, the more important such actions are, and the more difficult they are to undo, the greater is the
- individual's commitment to the belief.

- The belief must be sufficiently specific and sufficiently concerned with the real world so that events may
- unequivocally refute the belief.

- Such undeniably disconfirmatory evidence must occur and must be recognized by the individual holding the belief.

- The individual believer must have social support. It is unlikely that one isolated believer could withstand the kind of disconfirming evidence we have specified. If, however, the believer is a member of a group of convinced persons who can support one another, we would expect the belief to be maintained and the believers to attempt to proselyte or to persuade non members that the belief is correct. [34]

Festinger began by examining case histories, but then he was fortunate enough to be presented with ideal circumstances for observation and study; a millennial, or messianic, movement awaiting the end of the world on 21 December 1954, which they alone expected to survive.

Festinger et al were able to confirm his theory. When the world failed to end, the members chose to believe that earth had been given a second chance, and the group had now to spread a warning message worldwide. The group members increased their proselytizing dramatically, despite the failed prophecy.

In his book, *When Prophecy Fails*, Festinger explains that believers become motivated to reduce dissonance, or discomfort; to reconcile an inconvenient truth by altering existing cognitions, or adding new ones, in an attempt to create a consistent belief system. In the wake of a failed prophecy, believers may insist that the prophecy has happened, not in this world, but in some spiritual sphere.

This certainly holds true with the 1914 explanation of Christ's return propounded by the Governing Body of Jehovah's Witnesses. They began to insist that their prophecy had been fulfilled in a spiritual sense. They claimed that Jesus Christ began to rule as King in that year, setting up his kingdom in the heavens and ousting Satan, the Devil. (Revelation 12:7-12)

> "Jesus was granted still more authority in 1914. In that year he was appointed as King of Jehovah's Messianic Kingdom. When Jesus' rule began, 'war broke out in heaven.' The result? Satan and his demons were hurled to the earth, triggering an era of woe. The rampant wars, crime, terror, disease, earthquakes, and famines that have afflicted modern man remind us that Jesus is ruling in heaven right now." [35]

108

What about the "generation" that would not "pass away?" A *Watchtower*[36] article dated October 1, 1978 explains:

> "Thus, when it comes to the application in our time, the 'generation' logically would not apply to babies born during World War I. It applies to Christ's followers and others who were able to observe that war and the other things that have occurred in fulfillment of Jesus' composite 'sign.' Some of such persons 'will by no means pass away until' all of what Christ prophesied occurs, including the end of the present wicked system."(page 31)

With time on their hands, the Governing Body of Jehovah's Witnesses ruminated further on the meaning of the word, 'generation.' They came up with the idea that it signified a period of time coinciding with the lifetime of the average human. The "last days" would continue for no longer than a lifespan of seventy years, so the prophecy could still hold true. Seventy years onwards from 1914 takes us to the year 1984, but it is necessary to subtract about ten years to account for that generation's need to see the signs *and* recognize them. Those born in 1904 or thereabouts would see the fulfillment of the prophecy before they reached the age of seventy years old. Suddenly, the mid 1970s became very significant.

There was another avenue of approach to this calculation. According to the Organization's understanding of the Genesis account of creation, there are six creative 'days', each lasting seven thousand years, ending with the creation of Adam and Eve. (Genesis 1:31-2:3; Peter 3:8) Since then, we have been living in the Sabbath day resting period of another seven thousand years. Assuming that this Sabbath day would be complete at the end of Christ's one thousand year reign, the Day of Jehovah should occur six thousand years after the creation of Adam and Eve. It became imperative to establish when the first six thousand years of this resting period would likely come to an end, and when the seventh, Christ's thousand-year reign, would begin. In the 1960s the Watchtower Bible and Tract Society's publications began pointing to the year 1975.

"This seventh day, God's rest day, has progressed nearly 6,000 years, and there is still the 1,000-year reign of Christ to go before its end. (Rev. 20:3, 7) This seventh 1,000-year period of human existence could well be likened to a great sabbath day. . . In what year, then, would the first 6,000 years of man's existence and also the first 6,000 years of God's rest day come to an end? The year 1975." *Awake!* October 8, 1966, page 19

How was this year calculated? The book, *Life Everlasting in Freedom of the Sons of God*, pages 28-30, published in 1966 explains:

"In this twentieth century an independent study has been carried on that does not blindly follow some traditional chronological calculations of Christendom, and the published timetable resulting from this independent study gives the date of man's creation as 4026 B.C.E. According to this trustworthy Bible chronology six

110

thousand years from man's creation will end in 1975, and the seventh period of a thousand years of human history will begin in the fall of 1975 C.E."

However, in a *Watchtower* article two years later, a note of caution was sounded to the effect that there could be some small delay between the end of humankind's six thousand years of existence (autumn 1975) and the end of the world – corresponding to the interval between Adam's creation and that of Eve – but the faithful were given this assurance:

"Are we to assume from this study that the battle of Armageddon will be all over by the autumn of 1975, and the long-looked-for thousand-year reign of Christ will begin by then? Possibly, but we wait to see how closely the seventh thousand-year period of man's existence coincides with the sabbathlike thousand-year reign of Christ. If these two periods run parallel with each other as to the calendar year, it will not be by mere chance or accident but will be according to Jehovah's loving and timely purposes."

Significantly, the article commented,

"It may involve only a difference of weeks or months, not years." *The Watchtower*, August 15 1968, page 49

Imagine the impact all this must have had on all those who read and believed these pronouncements. If the end of the world, or "system of things" was truly imminent, what need was there for education, a career, marriage, and

111

raising a family? What need for insurance cover for homes or businesses? The devout eschewed these practicalities and concentrated on trumpeting what they believed to be the final warning to the wicked.

The *Awake!* magazine, May 22, 1969 had this to say:

> "If you are a young person, you also need to face the fact that you will never grow old in this present system of things. Why not? Because all the evidence in fulfillment of Bible prophecy indicates that this corrupt system is due to end in a few years. Of the generation that observed the beginning of the 'last days' in 1914, Jesus foretold: 'This generation will by no means pass away until all these things occur.' Therefore, as a young person, you will never fulfill any career that this system offers. If you are in high school and thinking about a college education, it means at least four, perhaps even six or eight more years to graduate into a specialized career. But where will this system of things be by that time? It will be well on the way towards its finish, if not actually gone! This is why parents who base their lives on God's prophetic Word find it much more practical to direct their young ones into trades that do not require such long periods of additional schooling... True, those who do not understand where we are in the stream of time from God's viewpoint will call this impractical. But which is really practical: preparing yourself for a position in this world that soon will pass away? or working toward surviving this system's end and enjoying eternal life in God's righteous new order?" (page 15)

The Kingdom Ministry, one of Jehovah's Witnesses' monthly publications for members, commended those who sold their homes and property in order to release funds to "pioneer," or proselytise full time, in the short time left.

"Reports are heard of brothers selling their homes and property and planning to finish out the rest of their days in this old system in the pioneer service. Certainly, this is a fine way to spend the short time remaining before the wicked world's end.–1 John 2:17." Kingdom Ministry, May 1974, page 3

Congregations flourished and grew as proselytes gathered together to await the coming wrath of God at Armageddon. Magazines brimming with grisly illustrations depicting the global holocaust to come, and exhortations to "let not your eye feel sorry" inured the faithful to the full horror that such pathological genocide would visit upon the ordinary citizens of planet earth. (Ezekiel 9:5,6)

Concern grew as 1975 and then 1976 came and went, and those who were alive in 1914 (and old enough to have understood its significance) steadily succumbed to old age and death. It became evident that something had gone seriously awry with the calculations. A reinterpretation of the first reinterpretation became necessary. The Governing Body of Jehovah's Witnesses rose to the challenge. Psalm 90:10, they pointed out, speaks of a human lifespan as seventy years "*or with special mightiness, eighty.*" So, legitimately, there could be a ten year delay. In the meantime, new guidance decreed that not all the "anointed" need be transported to heaven without seeing death. Some might be allowed to die, but as a class they would not all die before the advent of Armageddon.

However, as time went by, and the "anointed ones" continued to die an earthly death, it seemed prudent to reconsider the modified interpretation of what Jesus meant by "*this generation.*" The generation came to refer to anyone of the anointed class who was alive in 1914, regardless of whether they were old enough to understand its significance or not. These "anointed ones" would live on to see a "*great crowd of other sheep*" ushered into a clean earth after Armageddon. (Revelation 7:9) Somewhere around this time, they could expect to be lifted up, without seeing death, to take their seat in the heavenly kingdom.

Even those born in 1914 have now almost completely "passed away," so more readjustments of the last two reinterpretations have become necessary, over time. Incredibly, in 1995 the Governing Body of Jehovah's Witnesses transformed the interpretation of Jesus' words at Matthew 24:34, completely.

"Rather than providing a rule for measuring time, the term 'generation' as used by Jesus refers principally to contemporary people of a certain historical period, with

114

their identifying characteristics." *The Watchtower*, 1 November, 1995, page 17

Who then, comprised the generation that Jesus referred to? The publication continues,

"Therefore, in the final fulfillment of Jesus' prophecy today, 'this generation' apparently refers to the peoples of earth who see the sign of Christ's presence but fail to mend their ways." (page 19)

The Governing Body of Jehovah's Witnesses' new interpretation jettisoned nearly seventy years of teaching that the world will end during the lifetime of a generation of people who were alive to see the events of 1914. With neither regret nor apology, there was a complete *volte-face* and a reinterpretation of the data in order to claim that it was not referring to the righteous after all. "Wicked" people comprised the generation that would see the sign of his invisible presence but fail to act on it – presumably by becoming another one of Jehovah's Witnesses. What a turnaround!

But wait! Fifteen years later, yet another *volte-face* is introduced to congregations around the world via the April 15, 2010 *Watchtower* article, 'Holy Spirit's Role in the Outworking of Jehovah's Purpose.'

"...holy spirit is at work in bringing Bible truths to light. (Prov. 4:18) This magazine has long been used by "the faithful and discreet slave" as the primary channel for dispensing increased light. (Matt. 24:45) For example, consider our understanding of those who make up 'this generation' mentioned by Jesus. (Read Matthew 24:32-34.) To what generation did Jesus refer? The article 'Christ's Presence – What Does It Mean to You?' explained that Jesus was referring, not to the wicked, but to his disciples, who were soon to be anointed with holy spirit. Jesus' anointed followers, both in the first century and in our day, would be the ones who would not only see the sign but also discern its meaning – that Jesus 'is near at the doors.'

At this point, a new concept is introduced, that of 'overlapping.'

"What does this explanation mean to us? Although we cannot measure the exact length of 'this generation,' we do well to keep in mind several things about the word 'generation': It usually refers to people of varying ages whose lives overlap during a particular time period; it is not excessively long; and it has an end. (Ex. 1:6) How, then, are we to understand Jesus' words about 'this generation'? He evidently meant that the lives of the anointed who were on hand when the sign began to become evident in 1914 would overlap with the lives of other anointed ones who would see the start of the great tribulation. That generation had a beginning, and it surely will have an end. The fulfillment of the various features of the sign clearly indicate that the tribulation must be near. By maintaining your sense of urgency and keeping on the watch, you show that you are keeping up

116

with advancing light and following the leadings of holy spirit. – Mark 13:37."

In an attempt at clarification, the 2010 District Convention talk, 'Now is no time to leave the secret place,' explains that a generation consists of "contemporaries," that is, individuals who live at the same time.

Exodus 1:6 is used in support of this idea. Here, Joseph and "all his brothers" are referred to as "all that generation." So although their ages varied, these contemporaries were viewed as one generation. This is acceptable as far as it goes, but the reasoning takes an astonishing leap in logic to argue that in a similar manner the "generation" referred to at Matthew 24:34 comprises of two groups of anointed Christians. The first group comprises of those living in 1914 when "the sign" of Christ's presence began to be observed (Matthew 24:3), and the second group comprises of those who were anointed later. These two groups, for a time, are contemporaries. Jesus' words at Matthew 24:34, it is argued, indicate that some in the second group will witness the beginning of the "great tribulation."

In an attempt to bolster this claim, an instance is given in the form of F.W. Franz (one of the "anointed" class). Frederick W. Franz was born in 1893, baptized in 1913, and thus alive to discern "the sign" in 1914. Since Franz lived until 1992, any present-day anointed ones were contemporaries of his and are part of the "generation" that

Jesus said would not pass away, "until all these things occur."

Let's consider this objectively. Franz was born in 1893. The youngest member of the Governing Body, Geoffrey Jackson, was born in 1955. The Watchtower Bible and Tract Society reasoning encourages us to suppose that, since their lives 'overlapped' for a while, we should consider Frederick Franz and Geoffrey Jackson, born sixty-two years apart and unrelated, to be of the same generation. Looked at another way, it means that everyone who is alive today is of the same generation, since their lives overlap. Using this logic, your baby sister is of the same "generation" as your ninety-one year old great grandmother.

For the most common definition of a biblical "generation" you need look no further than the first chapter of Matthew 1:1-17. Here, *"All the generations then, from Abraham until David were fourteen generations, and from David until the deportation into Babylon fourteen generations, and from the deportation to Babylon until the Christ fourteen generations."* These generations are listed via their patriarchal fathers. There are no "overlaps."

In defense of their flexible approach to biblical interpretation, they reassure their flock with these words from the book of Proverbs 4:18:

> *"But the path of the righteous ones is like the bright light that is getting lighter and lighter until the day is firmly established."*

Having considered the above, would you conclude that the "light" has been getting brighter and brighter, or dimmer and dimmer? Let us not forget that countless individuals within a whole generation of people sacrificed everything, careers, marriages, children, even a home of their own, as a result of the Watchtower Society's interpretation of the "generation" scripture. To date, there has been neither apology nor even acknowledgement of these people's sacrifices by the Governing Body or any of its members. On the contrary, eerily reminiscent of the previously quoted May 1969 *Awake!* magazine, a recent *Watchtower* (June 15, 2012, page 23) urges,

> "If you are approaching the end of the schooling required of you, you may find yourself in good health and with few responsibilities. Have you seriously considered entering the regular pioneer ranks? No doubt, school counselors sincerely believe that it is in your best interests to pursue higher education and to plan for a secular career. Yet, their confidence lies in a social and financial system that has no lasting future. On the other hand, by pursuing a theocratic career, you will be pursuing truly worthwhile and lasting goals."

There has never been any objection within the rank and file of Jehovah's Witnesses to multiple changes of interpretation, despite the fact that those young people referred to in the 1969 article, who would "never grow old in this present system of things," are now over sixty years old and ready for retirement. Incredible as it might seem, all has been accepted and assimilated *without question*. Older Witnesses who have experienced these changes seem never to discuss them with younger members. It is difficult to imagine a society of people where changes of view would be accepted so willingly or without discussion, and with what Andrew Holden calls, "an unusual degree of complicity." [37]

A key reason for such bizarre twists and turns in biblical interpretation lies in the fact that the year 1914 is the lynchpin – the central tenet around which the whole modern day Organization of Jehovah's Witnesses has been built. Since that date, members have come to believe implicitly in the understanding that 1914 was the year in which God's kingdom was set up in the heavens and Satan, the Devil was cast down to earth. (Revelation 12:7-12) Revisiting verse 12, *"Woe for the Earth and for the sea because the Devil has come down to you, having great anger, knowing he has a short period of time,"* we can see that emphasis has always been placed on the "*short period of time*" indicated in this verse in order to support the notion that the "*last days*" for humankind will not be protracted.

Bearing in mind that 2014 marks the centenary of this "*short period of time*," it begs the question, did 1914 really mark the beginning of the "*last days*?"

1914

Throwing down my paintbrush, I leave my easel and cross the cold floorboards to the window. Outside, the sun's slanting rays illuminate the spring landscape. Low hills rise above the rutted fields. On the skyline, a leaden roof punctures cathedral clouds, dome-topped, shape-shifting, moving with the wind. The velvet flap of a pigeon swoops from barn to trees bursting with creamy white buds. Rising and dipping finches dart above the heads of black-faced lambs – miniature clouds, puffs of white and grey on grazing green.

Light. Colour. Shadow. Movement. Shimmering, glinting, nodding, swaying. I cannot paint its essence, yet I hope to capture something. Not a memory, for nothing has happened, and yet everything is in this moment. The window pane captures the pale ghost of me, looking inwards. I imagine a tiny image of myself reflected in the shining eyes of lambs skipping beyond the fence.

There is, of course, another sense of reflection. My father, keenly aware of what he terms, "the gentleman with the scythe" who follows close behind him, also reflects. He gazes down the long years and writes about his life. He sees himself reflected in the words he writes; the thoughts that shimmer and glint, nod and sway, the memories that shift and change as they sweep across the landscape of his mind. Does it matter if those memories are tinted – a flick of paint here, a broad brushstroke there? How he sees his life is surely the essence of himself.

The way he bows his head over his work, his left hand gently rubbing the crown of his head as he concentrates, reminds me of Grandfather. Perhaps my father is writing about him now.

I smile to myself, picturing Grandfather's aged, earnest face, alight with reminiscences. He served in the Napoleonic Wars, distinguishing himself under the Duke of Wellington at the Battle of Salamanca in 1812. Unfortunately, he spent the rest of his life thereafter talking endlessly about those wars, even when they were long past and superseded by others.

I recall a typical afternoon.

We're sitting in the study together. I'm attempting to sketch my grandfather while he reads his Bible, but he keeps breaking my concentration.

"Did you know that during the Napoleonic Wars, the three nations foretold in the Bible, Spain, Great Britain, and France, came head to head in a mighty battle for supremacy?" he asks me suddenly. "All the nations of Western Europe, including America and Russia, were involved - the longest international conflict in world history. Twenty-two years!"

I sigh and nod agreement, having heard these words many times before, and I know what is coming next.

"The casualties were horrific. Three to six million people worldwide. Think of that!" He picks up his magnifier and scans the print. "Listen to this! Proof that those wars fulfilled a crucial prophecy right here in the Bible." He taps the page vigorously with his forefinger.

"*'And as he sat upon the Mount of Olives, the disciples came unto him privately, saying, tell us, when shall these things be, and what shall be the sign of thy coming, and of the end of the world? And Jesus answered and said unto them, Take heed that no man deceive you. For many shall come in my name, saying, I am Christ; and shall deceive many. And ye shall hear of wars and rumours of wars: see that ye be not troubled: for all these things must come to pass, but the end is not yet'* – and this is the crucial bit – '*For nation shall rise against nation, and kingdom against kingdom.*'"

Grandfather throws his magnifier down with a triumphant gesture. "That's what Jesus prophesied, and so it has come to pass. There's no doubt that we are living in the 'time of the end.'"

"You need to rest, Grandfather," I coax, hoping to divert him, but aware that my strategy is weak and ineffective. "You know the doctor said that too much excitement would tax your heart, and now you're getting agitated."

"Nonsense! Never felt better!" he snorts.

With an inward sigh of resignation, I bend over his chair and fuss with the rough-spun blanket draped over his thin legs, tucking it in tightly.

"Now where was I?" he pauses, pretending to search his mind, but in truth, the scriptures are never far from the forefront of it. "Ah yes, the prophetic fulfillment of the words of Christ Jesus."

He picks up his Bible and magnifier again, his pale eyes glinting in the glow of the lamp I have placed on the small table next to him amongst his books.

'"*These are the beginnings of sorrows,*'" he reads, then pauses and looks up. '"The *beginnings* of sorrows,'" he repeats, leaning forward in earnest. "And haven't we seen such sorrows, my dear, just as he foretold?"

"Indeed we have, Grandfather," I respond, aware that this is a purely rhetorical question, for he's already nodding in agreement with himself.

Grandfather knows, of course, of my own father's involvement in the Crimean War and of the wounds he suffered on more than one occasion, but, unlike Grandfather, he will never speak of his experiences. I suspect his wounds are more than merely physical. I imagine it must be impossible to come through a war like that unscathed.

My own dear husband fought against the Russians in the Battle of Inkerman at Sevastopol as a serving officer in the 63rd Regiment. He's immensely fortunate to have survived the war relatively intact. Why, some people believed that the Crimean War itself was the Battle of Armageddon, and who can blame them?

I have to admit that it is not uncommon in our times for three generations of the same family to have been involved consecutively in warfare. I'm just thankful that Britain did not involve itself in the German Civil War and that country's war with France, or else it may have run to four generations, had my sons been conscripted. In truth, this century has been marked by incessant wars and bloody battles in one place after another.

I imagine that is why many prophets have arisen in our day, announcing that the end of all things has drawn near. I remember a Scottish clergyman, John Cumming, declaring that the world would end in 1862, and the Adventist, Jonas Wendell was convinced that the Second Coming of Christ would occur in 1873. The International Bible Students,[38] with which Grandfather seemed to have an affinity, predicted the end of the world no less than three times in the course of my own lifetime, in 1874, 1878, and again, only nine years ago, in 1881. No matter how many prophecies fail, they still seem to think that the end will come before the turn of the century. My own opinion, which is never asked for, is that I see the "end times" and Armageddon as a Sword of Damocles, forever suspended above the heads of the gullible by those wishing to dominate the lives of others.

I pick up my brush, my attention caught by the quality of light spilling across the landscape, and begin to paint.

***

Examining the painting

Ever since Jesus' violent death, his followers have been looking out for the signs he spoke of that would herald the beginning of the "last days." Jehovah's Witnesses are convinced that they commenced in the year 1914, but for this to be a correct interpretation of the prophecy, there has to have been a marked increase in each of its significators since 1914. Is there conclusive proof that this is the case?

Let's examine the picture Jesus painted, taking the "signs" in reverse order, to see whether they are more prevalent now than at any other time in human history. (Matthew 24:3-8; Luke 21:7-11; 2 Timothy 3:1)

"Nation will rise against nation and kingdom against kingdom." Matthew 24:7

"...and there will be great earthquakes, and in one place after another pestilences and food shortages." Luke 21v.11

"...and because of the increasing of lawlessness the love of the greater number will cool off." Matthew 24:12

Increasing lawlessness

Most people believe that crime is still on the increase, but statistical research does not support this assumption. Taking the statistics in Britain, for example, *The Economist*

October 20-26, 2012 (p.28) draws attention to the following facts:

"In the mid 1990s crime rates in Britain start[ed] falling sharply, reversing half a century of increases. Violence, burglary, robbery and car theft are all less common than they were ten years ago."

Young people are often targeted with the accusation that they are "rebellious," badly behaved, and turning increasingly to a lifestyle involving drugs, cigarettes, and alcohol. Again, the facts belie the myth. Below are a few extracts from the most recent report (2012) on drugs, smoking, and alcohol use, provided by the National Health Service in the United Kingdom.

Drugs
"There has been a decline in drug use by 11 to 15 year old pupils since 2001. In 2011, 17% of pupils had ever taken drugs, compared with 29% in 2001. There were similar falls in the proportions of pupils who reported taking drugs in the last year and the last month. The decline in the prevalence of drug use parallels the fall in the proportions of pupils who have ever been offered drugs, from 42% in 2001 to 29% in 2011."

Smoking
"A quarter (25%) of pupils had tried smoking at least once. This represents a sustained decline in the proportion of pupils who have tried smoking and is

lower than at any time since the survey began in 1982, when more than half of pupils (53%) had tried smoking.

"In 2011, 5% of pupils smoked regularly (at least once a week). The prevalence of regular smoking among 11 to 15 year olds has halved since its peak in the mid-1990s – 13% in 1996."

Alcohol
"Less than half (45%) of pupils aged between 11 and 15 have had at least one alcoholic drink in their lifetimes. The proportion of pupils in this age group who had never drunk alcohol has risen in recent years, from 39% in 2003 to 55% in 2011. The proportion of pupils who drank alcohol in the last week has fallen from 26% in 2001 to 12% in 2011." [39]

Mark Easton, Home Editor for the BBC was moved to comment on the above figures:

"No-one is suggesting that young people don't misbehave, but teenagers no longer seem to define themselves by wild disobedience. If anything, we are in the middle of a period of increasingly good behaviour." [40]

Hidden from public view, there are perhaps as many as 700,000 'young carers' in the United Kingdom alone – children between the ages of five and eighteen years old who look after friends, siblings, neighbors, and parents who need care.[41] According to the Carers Trust, 13,000 of these young carers take on care duties for over fifty hours a week.[42] Such behavior is not consistent with the prophetic claim that "*the love of the greater number will cool off.*"

Homicide rates

Despite the standard opinion that crime is ever-increasing, over the past century, homicide rates in five major European countries – Italy, Germany, France, Sweden, and England – show a long-term decline in homicide rates that lasted until the 1960s. A slight increase in that decade returned later to more peaceable levels once again.

Steven Pinker, examining government statistics pertaining to homicide for the period 1900-2010, comments,

"Every major Western European country showed a decline, and though it looked for a while as if England and Ireland would be the exceptions, in the 2000s their rates dropped as well. Not only did people cut down on killing, but they refrained from inflicting other kinds of harm. In the United States the rates of every category of major crime dropped by about half, including rape, robbery, aggravated assault, burglary, larceny and even auto theft. The effects were visible not just in the statistics but in the fabric of everyday life. Tourists and young urban professionals recolonized American downtowns, and crime receded as a major issue from presidential campaigns." [43]

In Pinker's opinion, this downward trend in lawlessness can only be satisfactorily explained with reference to what he describes as a 'Civilizing Process' – a wave of civilizing offensives, including revolutions in civil rights, women's rights, and children's rights.

> "..targeting of rape, battering, hate crimes, gay-bashing, and child abuse reframed law-and-order from a reactionary cause to a progressive one, and [the establishment's] efforts to make the home, work-place, schools, and streets safer for vulnerable groups... made these environments safer for everyone." [44]

Food shortages

In England, those who lived through the Great Famine of 1315-1318 could be forgiven for thinking that Jesus' prophecy concerning food shortages applied to their day. It is now understood that the early fourteenth century was entering a little Ice Age. Changing weather patterns brought heavy, drenching autumn rains that inundated the land and ruined harvests, followed by freezing winters under blankets of snow.

As a snapshot of the times, Michael Wood[45] describes the likely scene in Kibworth, England on a day in November

1315, when Robert of Gadesden arrived to collect rents from the local villagers.

> "When Robert rode into Kibworth from Oxford in November 1315 he saw a sorry sight: torrential rains had again devastated the harvest and this late in the year plough teams were still out on the Banwell Furlong along the steep baulks by the Leicester road. In the barns behind the houses he found widespread sheep rot; the pigs had 'leprosy and scab' and on one farm the cows had produced no calves. Each deluge swilled a brown tide down the Main Street, the 'King's Road', gathering in the muddy morass at the bottom in what the peasants called 'the marsh'. Among the village people there was also the 'flux', perhaps typhoid, and many were bedridden in their soaking houses."

The situation worsened, until,

> "Around Pentecost the rains started again and soon the pattern of catastrophe had set in across northern Europe as a whole as far as the Baltic Sea and the borders of Poland, where the Teutonic knights waged their interminable war on the Slavs."

In 1316 the situation in Britain was further exacerbated by a virulent cattle plague that broke out in Central Europe and now raged across the country striking down plough oxen from north to south of the country. At the same time, outbreaks of enteric dysentery and typhoid sent tens of thousands of people to their graves. Roughly 10% of the

131

population in England alone died between 1315 and 1318 – between half and three quarters of a million people.

Is there anything comparable to this in our time? Are food shortages an identifying feature of the period since 1914? According to the fact sheet, *2012 World Hunger and Poverty Facts and Statistics* provided by the World Hunger Education Service,[46]

"The world produces enough food to feed everyone. World agriculture produces 17 percent more calories per person today than it did 30 years ago, despite a 70 percent population increase. This is enough to provide everyone in the world with at least 2,720 kilocalories (kcal) per person per day, according to the most recent estimate that we could find. (FAO 2002, p.9)"

In the developing world, income is the factor that limits access to food, not the lack of supply, yet poverty is being tackled. For example, between 1990 and 2008 half a billion people in China have been lifted out of poverty.

"Over the past three decades, rapid economic development has contributed to an accelerated decline in absolute poverty in China. Both national and international indicators show that the number of people living in extreme poverty has been halved, leading to the achievement of one of the eight 2015 UN Millennium Development Goals (MDGs)."[47]

There are still problems to be addressed, but even so, the relative cost of eating is declining as the world's farmers are able to grow huge quantities of grain that can be processed quickly and shipped without spoilage.

Globesity

There are now more fat, well-fed people in the world than hungry people. Particularly since the 1990s, problems with overweight and obesity, dubbed "globesity," have become an escalating problem in many countries. In the United States, 35.5% of men and 35.8% of women are obese. In Britain, 26.2% of men and 26.1% of women are obese, and in Mexico, 24.2% of men and 34.5% of women are obese, according to figures published by the International Association for the Study of Obesity for the period 2009-2010. It is a leading, preventable cause of death worldwide – one of the most serious public health problems of the twenty-first century.

Overabundance and easy accessibility to processed food in convenience stores and supermarkets has been cited as a significant factor in globesity. Even in poor nations, high-fat, high-starch foods tend to be cheaper than fresh vegetables and fruits, so poor people eat more of them. According to U.N. figures, the consumption of oils and fats over the last thirty years has doubled and is forecast to keep on growing.

Retailers regularly stock very large sizes to accommodate the overweight. Patterns for sewing, knitting, and crochet now include instructions for much larger sizes than they did in the past. Public services must provide obese people with specialist equipment, such as wider chairs in waiting rooms, and even wheelchairs for those too obese to walk. Food portions in supermarkets and restaurants are getting larger to satisfy the appetite of obese people. Food producers are compelled to print the fat content of their products on the packaging in an effort to make consumers more aware of the content of their diets, as well as producing calorie reduced, half-fat and fat-free versions of their produce.

The current obsession with diet and obesity is unprecedented. Food is so abundant that almost anyone you care to speak to seems to be on one kind of diet or another. Visit any bookstore and you will find shelves groaning under the weight of books on the subject of diet. There are countless fitness clubs, societies, organizations, and individuals offering advice as well as diet and exercise programs for those anxious to shed their excess pounds.

How can this global situation possibly be ignored in order to accommodate the idea that Jesus' prophecy concerning 'food shortages' is being fulfilled in our day?

Famine and food shortages have been a prominent part of human experience for thousands of years, and so have the wars, political and social upheavals that have been responsible for so many of them. No matter which historic era we may choose to examine, famine and food shortages will have been a significant factor in the world of that time. But the truth is that food has never been as plentiful as it is now.

Pestilences

The Spanish Flu of 1918-19 and the AIDS epidemic are often presented as proof of the prescience of Jesus' words. The Spanish Flu pandemic, which ran from January 1918 to December 1920, wiped out between 20 and 50 million people. Claimed to be one of the deadliest natural disasters in human history, it accounted for 3% of the world's population.

AIDS made its appearance in the 1980s. According to one source,

"HIV has been estimated to have infected over 33 million people worldwide, the vast majority in Africa. Relatively few cases are seen in the developed nations, but they still number in the hundreds of thousands… 16.3 million people are said to have died from AIDS worldwide." [48]

This represents 0.2% of the world's population.

Awesome as these terrible diseases may be, can they be said to transcend in scale or frequency all other pestilences and diseases of previous centuries?

135

The Black Death

The Black Death, or Bubonic Plague mainly affects rodents, but their fleas can transmit the disease to people. We now know that once people were infected, the disease spread rapidly. 'Bubonic' refers to painful lymph node swellings called buboes, mostly found around the base of the neck, the armpits and groin. These swellings oozed pus and blood. The victim's skin became covered in painful swellings, turning from red to black,

> "...until finally, it might be, staggering out into the streets, they would fall and 'become a terrible and shocking spectacle for those who saw them, as their bellies were swollen and their mouths wide open, throwing up pus like torrents, their eyes inflamed and their hands stretched out upward, and over the corpses that lay rotting on corners, and in the porches of courtyards, and in churches, and everywhere, with no one to bury them'." [49]

Most victims died within four to seven days after infection.

In AD 541, the streets of Alexandria, Egypt became so polluted with rotting corpses piled up that it was impossible to bury them all. Those still alive and able to risk a venture outside to scavenge wore tags so that, in the event that they should succumb to the plague, any surviving family members could identify them.

When the plague reached Constantinople the following year, mounds of corpses littered the streets, forcing Emperor Justinian to give orders for them to be thrown into the sea.

> "...then, as the water turned into a soup of decomposing flesh, [Justinian ordered] vast pits to be dug on the far side of the Golden Horn. Within these, rows of bodies were laid and then 'trodden upon by feet and trampled like spoiled grapes,' so that further corpses, when they were hurled down from the rim of the pit, would sometimes vanish into the mulch. To those haunted by such a hellish vision, the entire world seemed to have become a winepress, in which countless multitudes were being crushed by the wrath of God."[50] (Revelation 14:19,20)

In the early 1330s another outbreak of this deadly plague struck China. Since China was one of the busiest trading nations in the world, it reached the shores of Europe in October of 1347 and spread swiftly across the continent, reaching as far afield as Scandinavia and Russia in the 1350s.

The same disease is thought to have returned to Europe every generation, with varying virulence and mortality, until the 1700s. During this period, more than a hundred plague epidemics swept across Europe, notably the Italian Plague of 1629-1631, the Great Plague of Seville (1647-1652), the Great Plague of London (1665–1666), and the Great Plague of Vienna (1679). Many cities lost more than

40% of their residents. Paris lost approximately 50% of its population, as did London.

Plague was endemic in London, with outbreaks in 1592, 1603, 1625-6, and 1636. In the 1626 plague, 40,000 lives were lost in the city, with death from plague manifest every year up to 1665, the year of the Great Plague.

In that year, Samuel Pepys, an English Administrator and Member of Parliament, who was one of those fortunate enough to survive, wrote in a letter to Lady Carteret:

The Great Plague of London in 1665 caused up to 100,000 deaths

"I have stayed in the city till above 7400 died in one week, and of them above 6000 of the plague, and little noise heard day nor night but tolling of bells; till I could walk Lombard Street and not meet twenty persons from one end to the other, and not fifty upon the Exchange; till whole families (ten and twelve together) have been swept away; till my very physician, Dr. Burnet, who undertook to secure me against any infection... died himself of the plague; till the nights (though much lengthened) are grown too short to

138

conceal the burials of those that died the day before, people thereby constrained to borrow daylight for that service; lastly, till I could find neither meat nor drink safe, the butcheries being everywhere visited, my brewer's house shut up, and my baker with his whole family dead of the plague." [51]

Venice, Hamburg, and Bremen are estimated to have lost at least 60% of their populations. Finally, after the Great Plague of Marseille in 1720–1722 and the 1771 plague in Moscow, it seems to have disappeared from Europe.

The Black Death lives up to its reputation for being one of the deadliest plagues in history. The total number of deaths worldwide from the pandemic has been estimated at 75 million people; an estimated 20-25 million deaths in Europe alone, wiping out between a third and two-thirds of Europe's population. It was a pandemic more than a hundred times more severe than AIDS, and far greater in scale and duration than even the Spanish Flu.

Smallpox

Although the Black Death finally died out, another devastating illness continued to wreak havoc on society in the eighteenth century. In Europe at this time, smallpox was a leading cause of death, killing an estimated 400,000 Europeans each year. During that century alone, smallpox killed an estimated 60 million Europeans, including five reigning European monarchs. Up to 30% of those infected, including 80% of children under five years of age, died from the disease and one third of the survivors became blind. By the mid-eighteenth century smallpox was a major endemic disease almost everywhere in the world except in Australia.

Smallpox continued to pose a major threat to health worldwide, until its eradication by a stringent global program of vaccination in the twentieth century (the last major outbreak in Europe was in 1972 in Yugoslavia). The global eradication of this devastating disease was certified on 9th December 1979 and subsequently endorsed by the World Health Assembly on 8th May 1980.

Typhus

Typhus is a disease caused by bacteria spreading through the bites of lice and fleas. The infection causes headache, fever, and a rash of red spots. It has plagued human populations throughout history. During the second year of the Peloponnesian War (430 BC), the city state of Athens in ancient Greece was hit by a devastating epidemic known as the Plague of Athens, which, according to David Durack and Robert Littman from the University of Maryland Medical Center, was probably typhus fever.

"Epidemic typhus fever is the best explanation. It hits hardest in times of war and privation, it has about 20 percent mortality, it kills the victim after about seven days, and it sometimes causes a striking complication: gangrene of the tips of the fingers and toes. The Plague of Athens had all these features." [52]

The plague returned twice more, in 429 BC and in the winter of 427/6 BC. With the death of the military leader, Pericles and 25 percent of the population, the Golden Age of Athens ended.

In Europe, there was a fearful epidemic in 1557-59, killing about ten percent of the population in England. A major epidemic occurred in Ireland between 1816 and 1819, and again in the late 1830s, and yet another major typhus epidemic occurred during the Great Irish Famine between 1846 and 1849.

Typhus epidemics made their appearance during the English Civil War, the Thirty Years' War and the Napoleonic Wars. When Napoleon invaded Russia, only one month into the campaign he had lost 80,000 soldiers to typhus and dysentery. During his subsequent retreat from Moscow in 1812, thousands more French soldiers died of typhus. The disease continued to be a major health problem in Russia until the early twentieth century. Great epidemics flared up whenever war or famine produced hardship and massive population movements.

K. David Patterson explains,

> "The worst typhus epidemics took place late in World War I and in the years of civil war following the Bolshevik Revolution. Typhus claimed some 2 to 3 million lives from 1918 to 1922."

Are we to conclude from this that pestilence is indeed a significant factor of society since 1914? Patterson continues,

"Incidence rates fell dramatically in the later 1920s and the disease had ceased to be a significant cause of death by 1940." [53]

Like smallpox, typhus was eventually brought under control by a vaccine developed in the twentieth century.

Malaria

Malaria is a tropical disease caused by a parasite, transmitted to human and animal hosts by the Anopheles mosquito. Symptoms include intense fever, chills, severe headache, muscle pains, nausea, and vomiting. If not promptly treated, infection may cause kidney failure, seizures, mental confusion, coma, and death.

DNA traces of *Plasmodium falciparum*, the deadliest and most frequent of the four pathogens that cause malaria, have been found in ancient Egyptian mummies more than 3,500 years old, thus identifying them as the earliest known cases of malaria. (The disease is also suspected of contributing to the death of the boy king, Tutankhamun.)

Although malaria was not always recognized as such in the ancient world, its symptoms have often been described, for instance, in ancient Chinese medical writings, and in the *Sushruta Samhita*, a Sanskrit medical

142

treatise. By the 4th Century BC it was widely recognised in Greece, and later, by Roman writers.[54]

Malaria decimated the armies of Napoleon and, in turn, it was a major contributing factor to the death of British troops in Walcheren, the Netherlands in 1809. [55]

There was no effective cure for malaria in Europe until the seventeenth century, when it is thought that South American Indians showed Spanish Jesuit priests how to extract quinine, a white powder-like substance, from the bark of the cinchona tree – a tree most often found in the Andes mountain range in Peru and Ecuador.

Today, according to WHO (World Health Organisation, April 2012), increasingly effective prevention and control measures have led to a reduction in malaria mortality rates by more than 25% globally since 2000 and by 33% in the WHO African Region – the region most vulnerable to the disease.

Stepping back from the canvas

When we take a step back and view pestilences and diseases over time, it becomes apparent that they were much more prevalent in the past than they are now. As we have seen, major twentieth-century medical advances have enabled the production of vaccines for smallpox, typhus, and many other formerly virulent diseases. While diseases are not completely eradicated around the world, we should be wary of holding up malaria or AIDS[56] as proof that we are living in the "last days."

On average, life expectancy is higher now than at any other time in human history. Between the years 1800 to 2000, life expectancy at birth rose from about 30 years of age to a global average of 67 and to more than 75 years in some countries. According to the latest figures from the Office for National Statistics, in 2010 the average life expectancy at birth across the United Kingdom for both men and women rose by another four months to 78.2 and 82.3 years respectively.

These figures are borne out by a series of reports published in the *Lancet*.[57]   A team headed by Dr. Christopher Murray of the University of Washington looked at 291 kinds of disease and injury around the world, to calculate life expectancy since 1970 and to count the number of deaths by disease from 1990 to 2010, with the purpose of aiding medical authorities to target their efforts more effectively.   An article in the *Economist*, commenting on Murray's work, summarizes:

"Murray's report is that the world is getting much healthier. The fundamental measurement of that – life expectancy at birth – has grown by leaps and bounds. Between 1970 and 2010 it rose, for women, from 61.2 years to 73.3. For men, who have always been more sickly, it went from 56.4 years to 67.5. In 1990 only 33% of those who died had passed their 70th birthdays. In 2010 that figure was 43%. In the intervening two decades 80

144

became the new 70. Nearly a quarter of 2010's deaths were of octogenarians. Some countries make enormous gains. Bangladesh, Bhutan, Iran, the Maldives and Peru, for example, all saw life expectancy jump by more than 20 years." [58]

One of the defining characteristics of the period since 1914 is not food shortage, pestilence, or disease, but a global increase in longevity and a massive reduction in the occurrence of pestilence.

Earthquakes: Are they on the increase?

"There will be great earthquakes, and there will be famines and plagues in many lands, and there will be terrifying things and great miraculous signs from heaven." Luke 21:11 (NLT)

Many Christians believe that earthquake activity is on the increase, but is this really true, or is it an illusion brought about by increased global communication – improved news coverage on radio, television, and internet – leading to greater awareness on the part of the public?

The British Geological Survey considers the question, Is Earthquake Activity Increasing? in an April 2010 article.[59]

"Recent devastating earthquakes in Haiti, Chile and China, as well as magnitude 7+ earthquakes in Indonesia and California, might give the impression that earthquake activity is increasing. In fact, a quick look at earthquake statistics over the last 20 years shows that this is not the case. On average there are about 15 earthquakes every year with a magnitude of 7 or greater.

"As with any almost random phenomena, the number of earthquakes each year varies slightly from this average, but in general, there are no dramatic variations. So far this year, there have been six magnitude 7+ earthquakes, in keeping with the annual rate."

The survey points out that one reason it might seem that there are more earthquakes is because of population expansion. In the past, when a large earthquake struck an isolated area, it went unnoticed and unrecorded, but as global population has increased, earthquakes are more likely to affect populated areas, hence more impact and greater news coverage.

A second reason for earthquakes to loom large in public consciousness is because earthquakes tend to cluster in time, as any quasi-random process does, although, in the long term, averages are reasonably constant. Clusters are obviously more noticeable than evenly spaced events, and periods of relative non-activity tend to get ignored.

A third reason for an apparent increase in earthquake activity is the fact that the ability of seismologists to detect and measure earthquakes has improved over the last few decades due to huge increases in the number of seismograph stations. These have recorded earthquake activity in many places where it would have remained undetected in the past.

The USGS Earthquake Hazards Program supports the view of the British Geological Survey. Under the heading, *Are Earthquakes Really on the Increase?* is the finding,

"Although it may seem that we are having more earthquakes, earthquakes of magnitude 7.0 or greater have remained fairly constant."

They emphasise that communication is key to understanding the perceived increase in seismic activity.

"Also, because of the improvements in communications and the increased interest in the environment and natural disasters, the public now learns about more earthquakes." [60]

What about the prospect of a future increase in activity? The survey comments,

"A long term increase in earthquake activity would require an increase in the Earth's internal energy supply, which would be difficult to account for."

It would seem that Jehovah's Witnesses and other Christians looking for data to support Jesus' prophecy scan the data from around 1900 to the present day and think they see an increase in seismic activity. In fact, what they are seeing is the effect of earthquake activity on an increasingly populous planet.

As Roger Musson, a seismologist with the British Geological Survey comments:

"If we compare the average global rates of large earthquakes, we find that these are stable as far back as we can trace them." He goes on to explain, "A big earthquake in California is news; a big earthquake in the Southern Ocean is noticed only by seismologists. So a run of earthquakes that by chance hit populated places makes it look as though the rate has increased, even if it hasn't."[61]

Still, concerns have been raised in some quarters that large earthquakes greater than 8.0 in magnitude have struck the earth at a record high rate since the year 2004. Peter Shearer, Professor of Geophysics at Scripps Institution of Oceanography and Philip Stark, Professor and Vice Chair of Statistics at the University of California, Berkeley examined the global frequency of large magnitude earthquakes from 1900 to 2011. They discovered that while the frequency of magnitude 8.0 and higher earthquakes has been slightly elevated since 2004, the increased rate was not statistically different from what might be expected from random chance.

"The recent elevated rate of large earthquakes has fueled concern that the underlying global rate of earthquake activity has increased, which would have important implications for assessments of seismic hazard and our understanding of how faults interact. We examine the timing of large (magnitude $M \geq 7$) earthquakes from 1900 to the present, after removing local clustering related to aftershocks. The global rate of $M \geq 8$ [greater than magnitude 8.0] earthquakes has been at a record high

148

roughly since 2004, but rates have been almost as high before, and the rate of smaller earthquakes is close to its historical average... Moreover, no plausible physical mechanism predicts real changes in the underlying global rate of large events. Together these facts suggest that the global risk of large earthquakes is no higher today than it has been in the past." [62]

Insurance companies have policies that cover natural disasters. Swiss Re, Munich Re, Hanover Re, and other companies conduct their own studies to monitor earthquake activity, and have discovered no statistical reason to alter their policies in order to accommodate an increase in earthquake activity. However, they also make it their business to study climate change, and recognize that it is a significant factor in assessing risk.

Following a Press Release, Peter Hoeppe, Head of Munich Re's Geo Risks Research Unit, told reporters in Munich recently,

"Climate change particularly affects formation of heat-waves, droughts, intense precipitation events, and in the long run most probably also tropical cyclone intensity." He added, "The view that weather extremes are becoming more frequent and intense in various regions due to global warming is in keeping with current scientific findings." [63]

Does it not strike you as strange that an acknowledged, significant global phenomenon like

149

climate change is given no mention in Jesus' predictions?

"Nation against nation"

"You will hear of wars and rumors of wars. See that you are not terrified, for the end is not yet. For nation will rise against nation and kingdom against kingdom...."

Jehovah's Witnesses insist that violence has increased significantly since 1914. Below is an extract from an article on their official website, 'Why They Resort to Violence.' [64]

"Yes, the violence we see today is a fulfilment of Bible prophecy about 'the last days.' Something else makes this an especially violent time. 'Woe for the earth and for the sea,' says the Bible, 'because the Devil has come down to you, having great anger, knowing he has a short period of time.' (Revelation 12:12) The Devil and his demon hordes have been cast out of heaven and are now concentrating their malevolence upon mankind. As 'the ruler of the authority of the air,' the Devil manipulates 'the spirit that now operates in the sons of disobedience,' making the earth an increasingly violent place. – Ephesians 2:2."

If violence is truly on the increase to a degree so significant that it has never been experienced before, then people prior to 1914 must have lived safer, less violent lives – and this would have had to be true of all periods of time throughout the centuries since Jesus' prophecy was first uttered.

Why then, in the centuries following the death of Christ, do we see the continuing need for massive city defenses; towering city walls, gates, battlements, fortresses, bastions, buttresses, castles, ditches, moats, and watchtowers? Historically, individuals and tribes of people gained ascendancy through tyranny and strength of arms; armed gangs and invaders swept across the land time and again, using intimidation and force to impose their will on the world around them. They subjugated and exploited their citizens and treated their country as plunder. Protest met with the summary execution of individuals and protestors *en masse*. Unscrupulous rulers have almost invariably been obsessed with the acquisition of wealth and power, so it is not surprising that the annals of history bear testimony to constant wars, civil wars, and bloody conflicts.

In *The Better Angels of our Nature*, psychologist, Steven Pinker addresses the phenomenon of violence and provides compelling data to prove that overall, despite the great wars of the last century, we are far safer now than in any other time in human history. He argues that, far from increasing, violence is actually decreasing. In fact, "today we may be living in the most peaceable era in our species' existence." This might seem counter-intuitive, but consider this question: If you were to travel back in time, how safe would you expect to be?

A journey to ancient Rome might seem appealing, but estimates for the Fall of Rome (circa 400AD) account for

151

the loss of some 8,000,000 people. Taking the death toll as a proportion of world population at the time, this is equivalent to roughly double the death toll for the Second World War. Civilization was destroyed throughout the entire Roman Empire. By the year 700AD, there was almost no vestige left of the once great Roman civilization.

According to Matthew White,[65] the eighth century AD witnessed the worst atrocity of all time. The An Lushan Revolt and Civil War, a rebellion spanning eight years during China's Tang Dynasty, resulted in the loss of 36,000,000 people, or two-thirds of the empire's entire population according to censuses. That accounts for a sixth of the world's population at that time. Compare this with World War II, which, though horrific, accounted for an estimated one twenty-fifth (3.17%-4%) of the world's population.

In the thirteenth century, the Mongols (eventually known as the Tatars) carried out such revolting massacres that they are viewed by some historians as the most savage conquerors in history. In 1219 their first leader, Genghis Khan personally took control of a three-pronged attack against the Khwarizm Dynasty.

"The Mongols swept through every city's fortifications with unstoppable savagery. Those who weren't immediately slaughtered were driven in front of the Mongol army, serving as human shields when the Mongols took the next city. No living thing was spared, including small domestic animals and livestock. Skulls of men, women, and children were piled in large, pyramidal mounds." [66]

A few days after a massacre, soldiers were sent back into the devastated cities to search for any survivors hiding in the ruins. These were mercilessly slain. According to the 'worst-things' list, the Mongol Conquests between 1279 and 1368 took an estimated 40,000,000 lives. This is ten times as devastating as Word War II, proportional to the population alive at the time.

Time travelers visiting Europe in the Middle Ages, an era romanticized in fantasy fiction, would be distressed to find it no less fraught with violence and danger, especially for women. Punishments and tortures reserved exclusively for women included the Scold's Bridle and the ducking stool, as well as the prospect of capital punishment for witchcraft. Medieval Christendom was "a culture of cruelty."

"Torture was meted out by national and local governments throughout the Continent, and it was codified in laws that prescribed blinding, branding, amputation of hands, ears, noses and tongues, and other forms of mutilation as punishments for minor crimes. Executions were orgies of sadism, climaxing with ordeals of prolonged killing such as burning at the stake, breaking on the wheel, pulling apart by horses, impalement through the rectum, disembowelment by winding a man's intestines around a spool, and even

153

hanging, which was a slow racking strangulation rather than a quick breaking of the neck." [67]

Drawing closer to this century, do the sixteenth and seventeenth centuries promise a safer and less violent environment? On the contrary, the period between 1560 and 1715 in Europe was marked by relentless religious persecution filled with violent reprisals and counter reprisals. The slaughter of Huguenots (French Protestants) by Catholics at Sens, Burgundy in 1562 marked the beginning of more than thirty years of religious antagonism between French Protestants and Catholics. In turn, Huguenots, when they gained control, persecuted their Catholic opponents with equal ferocity. Atrocities included strangulation, burning at the stake, severing limbs, disembowelment, hanging, and burying alive. Many of these events did not take place in secret, but were attended by eager crowds of onlookers. In fact, the hanging of criminals was generally viewed as legitimate entertainment for families to watch, including small children.

Consider the seventeenth century English Civil War, fought between 1642 and 1651. Historical records count 84,830 dead as a direct consequence of that war. This figure doesn't seem overwhelming until you realize that it represents a 3.7 percent loss of population over less than a ten-year span. Set against a British loss of 2.19 percent of population at the time of the First World War and a 0.94 percent loss of population at the time of the Second World

War over twenty years later, the devastating effect of the Civil War singles it out as a particularly bloody passage in English history.

During the eighteenth century, the Age of Enlightenment saw movements to abolish slavery, dueling, torture, and even cruelty to animals, but there was little advancement in the prevailing attitude towards domestic violence. Wife-beating was not only widely tolerated, but sanctioned by English common law, which stipulated that a man may discipline his wife and children with a stick or whip, as long as it was no wider than his thumb. This violent "rule of thumb" prevailed in England and America until the late nineteenth century.

Taking a more global view, the astounding catalog of atrocities committed by the British, Spanish, Portuguese, and French abroad during their lengthy and often bloody campaigns for the acquisition of territory and resources is well documented. Genocide and ethnic cleansing took place in one country after another across the globe right up to the twentieth century. A particularly horrific figure is involved in the colonization of North America from the fifteenth to the nineteenth century, which took an estimated 20,000,000 American Indian lives.

1914 - today

In view of this long history of man's inhumanity to man, does it make sense to claim that conditions are worse today than at any other time in human history? The years

155

since 1914 do not reflect Jesus' prophecy concerning the "signs." On the contrary, we have examined evidence to show that lawlessness is decreasing, and scientific advances in medical care and the eradication of chronic disease is increasing life expectancy.

We have observed that people are instinctively loving and kind to members of their own tribe, but are inclined to distort and demonize the reputations of people of other tribes. This leads to periodic outbreaks of violence against them. One of the goals of the Enlightenment, and of moral people today, is to try to broaden the definition of what we consider to be our own 'tribe.' We endeavor to expand the concept of 'tribe' and the geographical area it covers. Our ultimate goal is to reach a situation where all humans imagine and behave as if they were in the same tribe, so that all people display their instinctive loving and caring attitude for one another universally. We also strive to rise above the instinctive tendency to view other tribes and groups as inferior, and thus minimize violence and prejudice.

This is a process that has been going on for hundreds of years. Defensive town walls and castles with their gates, battlements, and moats fell into disuse as people began to expand their view of 'tribe' to cover all people living in the same country. Today, ancient city defenses are considered picturesque tourist attractions; quaint reminders of the violence of a bygone age. In other words, the cumulative effect of the gradual expansion of our definition of 'tribe' has resulted in a long-term reduction in violence, and there is every reason to endorse the argument that modern cultural institutions are continuing to modify our behavior and attitudes, making us better people with a social conscience that abhors violence.

Instances include:

- The change in attitude towards capital punishment and public executions. In most civilized countries, these are a thing of the past. As a result, those who have abolished the death penalty have benefited from lower crime rates than those who have not done so.

- Ethnic minorities, women, and children are less likely to be victims of violence in many parts of the world, and this is likely to be an ongoing trend.

- Insular tribal attitudes are in the process of being replaced by the concept of a global family.

- Peaceful restoration of independence for many countries, e.g. Singapore, Australia, New Zealand, and Canada. India, too, gained independence in 1947 after peaceful, non-violent resistance.

- In democratic countries, society demands better behavior from its leaders. They understand that they are not above the reach of law because

157

representation and accountability work towards driving up standards and ensuring that persons in positions of authority act responsibly, or else face public censure.

- In the European Union, neighboring countries such as France and Germany have developed a firm determination to avoid another conflict like the Second World War. They work hard to maintain friendly relations through trade, economic and business links.

- A growing number of nations around the world have reached the rational and sane perception that, rather than resorting to violence, they can work to find acceptable solutions to disagreements through peace-keeping envoys, endeavoring to bring together all parties involved around the negotiating table. Northern Ireland is a recent case in point.

As a consequence of advances like these in democracy, there are fewer wars with fewer fatalities.

Taking a broader, more objective view of human civilization throughout the ages, it is possible to formulate an entirely different attitude towards our current century. The question we should be asking now, according to Pinker, is not, "Why is there war?" but, "Why is there peace?"

THE DAY

From her vantage point at the casement window, Carla gazed out across a sea stripped of color and movement. The sun lay hidden behind a bank of angry cloud, flickering on the western horizon, but as yet the wind was still. A sluggish tide was on its way in, smothering the rocks that surfaced and submerged in the crestless swell. It skimmed across the narrow strip of sand below, obliterating its litter of lugworm casts and scattering solitary seabirds patrolling the shoreline.

On these remote islands, it was hard to imagine that across the ocean a deadly virus had swept across the land with frightening speed, wiping out human life wherever it was found. It seemed to hit everywhere at once around the globe, indistinguishable from a common cold at first, but rapidly overcoming its victims. Scarcely more than six months after the outbreak there were no survivors, bar the Servants of God. They were the sole inhabitants of this remote string of islands, protected by their self-sufficiency and isolation. It was God's handiwork, of course; His means of cleansing the earth of all its wickedness. The judgement of Armageddon.

Or so Carla had believed, until Amy went missing.

Clara remembered the series of events as if a film was playing in her head. As reports of the rising death toll came in from around the world, Clara's anxiety for her childhood friend increased. Where was she? Could she have gone to the mainland for some reason, and now found herself trapped there? Usually bubbly and cheerful, Amy had been acting strangely just before the virus hit. Clara asked if she had done anything to offend her, but Amy had just shaken her dark curls and told her, no, everything was just fine. Nevertheless, she had become increasingly morose, and it was painfully obvious that she was beginning to avoid Clara. Then she had disappeared. Clara was baffled.

Shortly after her disappearance, Clara searched her room for any clue as to what had happened to her, but there was nothing. A few days passed before she finally remembered that Amy had kept a diary hidden behind a loose skirting board beneath the bed. How could she have forgotten it, the one source of information that might provide her with answers! But would Amy have left it behind? Clara hurried back to the room, fearful that either Amy had taken it with her, or the room had been stripped and cleaned and the diary discovered. With a sigh of relief, she found it still tucked away in its hiding place, dusty, but intact.

What she read in that diary was the reason she was here now, in an ante-room of the Servants of God's headquarters, awaiting the judicial verdict of the Older Men. Not that there had been a trial as such – more a kind of dialogue, in which she confronted them with her findings, and they dismissed her objections.

"Seven signifies completeness, Clara," they had told her. "Seven servants or angels of God have carried out

God's vengeance upon the seven continents, just as prophesied in Revelation chapter sixteen, verse seventeen, *'The seventh angel poured out his bowl into the air, and out of the temple came a loud voice from the throne, saying, "It is done!".'* It is God's completed judgement against the wicked peoples of the earth."

So it was true. Amy's diary recorded that she was one of seven Servants of God chosen by the Older Men to carry a fatal influenza virus to the seven major continents of the world – Europe, Africa, Australia, Asia, Antarctica, and northern and southern America. Amy had been dispatched to Milan. She was an expendable pawn in these men's death-dealing game.

All through those terrible months, as reports of the death toll kept rising, Clara had sat by the radio, not knowing what else to do. There was nobody she could turn to with this damning information. Even if she showed them the diary, nobody would believe her, she was sure of that. They would dismiss it as the fantastical imaginings of a pubescent teenager. Besides, the damage was already done. It was too late.

Clara was devastated. It was not Divine Judgement after all. God was not striking down the world and destroying it. It was the handiwork of the Servants of God.

The Servants, under the direction of the Older Men, had sold their properties on the mainland, bought up these islands, and gathered their people together from across the globe. Everyone who had not heeded the call lay dead along with the rest. She had thought it all God's divine plan. She had believed the same as all the others. Now her devotion and unwavering obedience seemed naïve and irresponsible. How could she live with the knowledge that the Older Men had committed mass genocide, wiping out the entire population of the earth – billions upon billions of people?

"We received brighter light from God, modifying our previous understanding of the scriptures in Revelation," one of the twelve assembled Older Men explained with a patriarchal smile, "just as it says in God's word, '*The path of the righteous is like the first gleam of dawn, shining ever brighter till the full light of day.*'"

How did they manage to get their hands on such a virus, and why had none of the ordinary members of the Servants of God been informed? Clara had demanded. Surely they had a right to know the truth?

"God reveals His purpose only to a select few, just as at the Last Supper Jesus revealed certain truths only to his closest disciples," she was told with quiet assurance. "As His true modern disciples, we were entrusted with a divine commission. You must understand that God has cleansed the earth of the wicked, just as He promised, but He has used us as His holy instruments to carry out His will. There is no difference. The end result is the same."

Clara was silent. She remembered a dream in which she stood on the pinnacle of a church steeple at a dizzying height above the earth. One step in any direction and she would plummet to her death.

An Older Man gestured towards the distant mainland.

"Once all the corpses have decomposed or been picked clean by scavengers, we will be able to reoccupy the mainland and establish God's righteous New Order worldwide." He paused to give her the full benefit of his frown. "But there will be no room for rebels and dissenters." He leaned forward suddenly.

"*He* – or she – *who is not for us, is against us.*"

Now, waiting in the ante-room, Clara watches a seagull swoop across the sea, its body luminous against the darkening sky. As it dips towards the swell, the door behind her clicks open and the Older Men file in.

***

"The whole world is lying in the power of the wicked one"
(1 John 5:19)

Jehovah's Witnesses are serving with "the day of Jehovah's anger," Armageddon, in mind. (Zephaniah 2:2) They consider themselves, "temporary residents" in a world run by Satan. Their Organization's understanding of where they are in the timeline of biblical prophecy is responsible for the pessimistic attitude towards the world displayed by Jehovah's Witnesses. They believe, *"The world is passing away and so is its desire, but he that does the will of God remains forever."*

As Jehovah's Witnesses believe that only those who are dedicated, baptized members of their Organization will be saved at Armageddon, we need to stop for a moment and consider what this really means.

If we take the United Kingdom as an example, the population at the time of publishing stands at approximately 60 million people. There are about 120,000 Jehovah's Witnesses in the UK, representing 0.2% of the population. What they pray for and expect to happen at Armageddon is that 99.8% of the entire population will be slaughtered by the hand of God, so that 0.2% can occupy the land. This alone would constitute an appalling act of violence, far worse than that committed by any other regime in human history.

Worldwide, Jehovah's Witnesses pray for and expect upwards of 6,993,000,000 people to be destroyed directly by God himself. That constitutes 99.9% of the entire population of the world. 7.4 million Jehovah's Witnesses expect to stand by and watch as their God, Jehovah wreaks his vengeance upon humankind until everyone who is not a dedicated, baptized member of the Organization of Jehovah's Witnesses is annihilated. At the end of the Day of Jehovah at Armageddon, the earth will be littered from end to end with the corpses of men, women, little children, and babies - soaked red with their blood.

Surely it will constitute a mammoth task for Jehovah's Witnesses to bury all the corpses? Not at all, because according to the Bible (Revelation 19:17), the birds will assist in disposing of them.

"And I saw an angel standing in the sun, who cried in a loud voice to all the birds flying in midair, 'Come, gather together for the great supper of God, so that you may eat the flesh of kings, generals, and mighty men, of horses and their riders, and the flesh of all people, free and slave, small and great.'"

What will the survivor's reaction be to all this gruesome slaughter? Surely, such a spectacle will cause distress? The following extracts are from The Watchtower Bible and Tract Society publication, '*The Nations Shall Know That I Am Jehovah*' - *How?* (1971). Pages 376-377 give us some insight into their thinking on the matter.

"This feast for the birds of every sort and for the wild beasts is called a 'sacrifice' by Jehovah, for sacrifices made to him in pre-Christian times called for the slaughter of animal and bird victims. Their blood has to flow. In Revelation 19:17 it is called 'the great evening meal of God.' The offering of communion sacrifices or peace offerings to Jehovah used to be the occasion for feasting on part of the victim's flesh by the offerer and his kinsmen. In the sacrificial feast that Jehovah spreads for the birds and wild beasts by his glorious victory over [Satan's] crowd, Jehovah places no bar upon them against drinking the blood of the slain humans, a thing forbidden to human creatures from Noah's day onward. (Genesis 9:1-4) This spells great reproach for the executed ones of [Satan's] crowd. When, for instance, the scavenger dogs

165

of Jezreel devoured the carcass of wicked Queen Jezebel, they left only some bones to be buried. – 2 Kings 9:30-37"

Heaps of bones will still present a potential problem for the Armageddon survivors.

"The fact that Jehovah leaves the bodies of those slain at the defeat of [Satan's] attack lying exposed on the ground for birds and wild beasts to gorge themselves upon symbolizes that they will not be laid in respected memorial tombs in hope of a resurrection for them. The unburied dead, 'those slain by Jehovah,' will be so enormously many that even the carrion birds and scavenging wild beasts could never take care of their consumption. The burial of even what remains after these lower creatures have their fill would be stupendous."

But Jehovah's Witnesses need not suffer stress worrying about it. The Governing Body of Jehovah's Witnesses is confident in their God's ability to handle the problem.

"Doubtless the Almighty God will use some highly scientific means, whether including antimatter or not, to dispose of the surplus of decaying bodies in a speedy and sanitary way. This remains for the survivors of the 'war of the great day' to see and witness. We remember that Noah and his seven fellow survivors of the global Deluge were not burdened with burying the human victims of that world catastrophe after they came out of the ark and renewed Jehovah's worship on earth. – Genesis 8:18-22."

166

The publication informs prospective survivors on what their attitude should be towards the fate of 99.9% of the entire earth's inhabitants.

> "'How horrible all this!' Should that be our reaction of mind toward this prophecy of the disastrous defeat of Gog's dastardly attack upon the only remaining peaceful worshipers of Jehovah on earth at the end of this violent system of things? Not rightly so!" para. 23

Concerning the bizarre speculation about the disposal of corpses, this was endorsed more recently in a 2007 convention talk, 'You Will Be With Me in Paradise,' given by Ciro Aulicino, a representative of the Watchtower Society and member of Bethel headquarters.

> "However, when Armageddon is over, we are going to face a rather gruesome, well not a rather, a very gruesome situation. Let's turn to Jeremiah 25 and see what he says about it through his prophet, Jeremiah in chapter 25 verse 33:
> *'And those slain by Jehovah will certainly come to be in that day, from one end of the earth clear to the other end of the earth. They will not be bewailed, neither will they be gathered up or be buried. As manure on the surface of the ground, they will become.'*
> "Try to picture this, friends. This gruesome picture. Dead bodies and body parts of the wicked will lie strewn on the surface of the ground, in streets, alleyways, fields, and buildings. Now notice that God in this verse tells us here that no one will mourn or bury these dead ones. Now

167

what does this tell us? It shows us that we will not be traumatized by His mass annihilation of these individuals. No, this divine execution of the wicked will not haunt us for the rest of our lives. Rather, we will react to it today as we do when a vicious serial murderer is executed – how do you feel about him when he gets it? Why, we will feel an inner satisfaction! Our indignation has been appeased. Yes, a sense of triumph that at last, Jehovah's justice has been served. AIDS has been stopped. The gays are gone. The homosexuals, the lesbians, the murderers, the drug lords – all gone. Are you going to feel sorry for these people? [*speaker chuckles*] No. And those that don't mind them living around – you gonna feel *sorry* for individuals? No! "Now how will Jehovah dispose of these bodies of those slain by him? Ezekiel 39 and Revelation 19 – you can look this up at home, we haven't got the time – tells us that he will beckon his wild beasts and birds to come and devour their fleshy parts. However, the vast numbers of cadavers will be much more than they can consume. Therefore, Jehovah will doubtless use a highly scientific means at his disposal, perhaps antimatter, to disintegrate the putrefying organisms. Now, especially in cities where we live, there is going to be a high concentration of dead ones. We're going to have to need them, because the animals in the Bronx zoo, if they got out, still couldn't eat all the bodies in the Bronx! [*speaker and audience laugh*]"

This public address sounds like the ravings of a madman – but one whose views are endorsed by the thousands of

168

people who attended that assembly, and by millions of Jehovah's Witnesses worldwide.

Once all trace of the dead has been obliterated, the survivors expect to take over the best of the houses left by the deceased and live forever on earth, free from wickedness. (Micah 4:4)

A few questions still need clarification. For instance, what will happen if, in that New Order, children who were traumatized by the bloodbath of wholesale slaughter voice their objection to such brutality and question God's actions? Also, what will happen to any person or persons who do not conform to the tenets of the New Order? How will they be dealt with?

An article from the Jehovah's Witnesses Official Website explains that after the Day of Jehovah at Armageddon, there will be a thousand-year-long judgement period:

"[It] will give billions of [resurrected] people their first opportunity to learn about God's will and to conform to it. This means that a large-scale educational work will take place. Indeed, 'righteousness is what the inhabitants of the productive land will certainly learn.' (Isaiah 26:9) However, not all will be willing to conform to God's will. Isaiah 26:10 says: 'Though the wicked one should be shown favor, he simply will not learn righteousness. In the land of straightforwardness he will act unjustly and will not see the eminence of Jehovah.' *These wicked ones will be put to death permanently.* – Isaiah 65:20" (Italics mine)[68]

In other words, having witnessed the slaughter of between six and seven billion people, Jehovah's Witnesses will be prepared to carry out further executions, even on members of their own small band of survivors.

Is it possible to create a Utopia by force, under threat and by acts of violence? Can a paradise exist in which the death penalty has been reintroduced world-wide with the overt intention of eradicating the "wicked" sin of independent thought? The above article does not address the issue of how dissenters are to be put to death or who is going to carry out the death sentence, but the implications are sinister, to say the least. Only complete indoctrination and the firmly held conviction that everyone outside their Organization is wicked and deserving of death, can explain the placid contemplation of such bloodletting.

Jehovah's Witnesses believe themselves to be a separate people, the apple of God's eye. They believe they have been cherry-picked by him as his favored people. They alone are worthy of inheriting everlasting life in perpetual youth on an idyllic earth, while the rest of humanity, lacking God's favor, is swept away to make room for them. They have rationalized their tribalism in the same way as the Israelites. The God who decreed, "Thou shalt not kill," (Exodus 20:13) issued explicit instructions to the Israelites to do just that, on a massive scale (e.g. Exodus

170

22:20; 1 Samuel 15:3). How can this dichotomy be justified? If we attach to, *"Thou shalt not kill,"* the words *anyone who is a fellow Israelite,* we have our answer. The Israelites were God's chosen people, the ones favored by God. All other peoples already occupying Palestine at that time were considered enemies of God and could be slaughtered wholesale if they put up any kind of resistance to the Israelites' sweeping occupation of the land.

Similarly, all who are not fellow Witnesses are considered enemies of God, candidates for mass execution, while Jehovah's Witnesses, under the sheltering canopy of their God's protection, expect to take possession of the whole earth.

NEW ORDER

Everywhere is the faint smell of burning, smouldering ash and charred earth. Our vehicle rumbles past row upon row of drab tenement blocks, just like the one we have come from, all of them occupied by The Risen. The road is bumpy and potholed, and the land is arid and featureless. Even the birds seem to have abandoned this place. I do not recognize this landscape, even though I know it is the same land, the same island where I was born thousands of years ago, but everything is different now.

When I first awoke, strangers told me that I had been given life again, had been reborn, but they would not tell me where to find my husband and my two sons. I was told that they are in another place, and that I am not to think about them. I must not think about turning to the Goddess for comfort either. I must not worship her or think about her because the god who raised me can read my heart and he will punish me.

One of the strangers tells me she is from my own time, but she, like most of the others in the block, comes from Crete. I only know of its existence because my husband described to me a magnificent royal palace built there. I recognize none of the Cretans. They all seem to be as frightened as I am, and refuse to talk about the past. Why are we here? What do they intend to do with us? The Risen whisper amongst themselves and talk in low voices, but nobody seems to know anything for certain. They ache with loneliness, just like I do. All the tenement blocks are the same, full of bereft, displaced people, men and women housed in separate blocks. It is a terrible place. There are no children here; no sound of laughter, or music, or a snatch of song.

In the daylight hours, the men are taken away in wheeled vehicles and put to work, building more tenement blocks and repairing roads. None of them are sent down to the harbors to fish. Low buildings have been erected where we, the Risen women, make the suffocating garments that Jehovah's Worshipers favor. The woman, the stranger, tells me we are privileged to share in such a vital good work. We do not talk openly. We keep our heads bowed, and speak only when spoken to by the supervising Worshipers. In return, clothing and food is given us, but there is never much fish.

Those that put us in the tenement blocks are all worshipers of the male god, Jehovah. They don't understand our language. They are called "Armageddon Survivors," or "Approved by God." What does that mean? I think it means they do not live inland in tenement blocks like us, The Risen. Instead, they live close to the sea in whitewashed houses with painted doors and windows of deep blue. They have pots of crimson flowers on their doorsteps and streets shaded with trees laden with fruit, and vines of purple blossom.

More than that, they have families.

Where is my husband? My dear sons? Are they even on this accursed island? If I could only find them, maybe we could escape. Seize a boat and go – where? Where could we hide, away from the face of the Worshipers' god?

I dread each day. When my eyes open in the morning they fill with tears because I remember that I am one of the Risen. My heart sinks. This island is not my home anymore. Its heart is ripped out, just like mine. It is a dead place. The home of my heart lies in the distant past, buried beneath the centuries, swaddled in the shroud of the Goddess.

The Worshipers seem to think that we should be eternally grateful for being raised from the dead to life again, but they have no understanding. All the myriad concerns and activities that made up our daily lives have been taken away from us. Our culture, our traditions, our communities, our temples, our homes, and our families are all gone; everything that made us who we were. Now we are just lost souls in substitute bodies; alive, but not living. We are hollow shells, ghosts of ourselves, without hope, without destiny, without comfort.

We are forced into meaningless labor, coerced into learning another language, and reading a black book full of indecipherable marks. We are herded into cramped vehicles and taken to endless meetings where we are expected to worship the very god responsible for our miserable condition.

Even so, it is not wise to complain. Some of those who have done so have been taken away and have not returned. It is believed that they must be imprisoned somewhere, or maybe executed as rebels. There are rumors circulating that there was a group of dissidents, survivors of the war, hiding in caves somewhere along the coast, but that they were dragged out and killed, even the women and children.

The vehicle in which we are traveling to yet another interminable meeting bumps and sways as it rounds a corner. My unfamiliar clothing is clinging to my body and I can feel sweat trickling down my back. I do not sleep well in my tenement cell, but now I feel my eyelids grow heavy, and my head droops forward...

I am walking down the street towards the harbor, the sun hot on my back and my bare shoulders. The cobalt sea is dancing with a thousand jewels as a small fleet of crescent-shaped fishing boats bustles with men making preparations to leave, raising their square sails against the beaming sky. Sturdy oarsmen stripped to the waist swarm on board and settle into their places. At a word, they dip their oars into the crystal waters, raise and dip them again in one, fluid movement. My husband and my two sons, each commanding his own vessel, raise a hand to me and grin, as they always do when I come to see them set sail. My heart swells with pride. They are lithe and handsome, their bodies brown and glistening in the sunlight. They are masters of their trade. As the boats leave the sheltering walls of the harbor, gulls rise up to wheel and scream in their wake, knowing that when they return their nets will be filled with tuna. A billowing mist rolls in, blotting out the horizon, and blanketing the sea. The fleet sails into it and is lost to sight...

We have stopped outside the male god, Jehovah's temple and we alight and make our way inside. Even though the Worshipers smile and show us to our seats, there is no feeling of belonging. The interior is nothing like the beautiful temple of the Goddess, where I once worshiped and took my turn officiating at her altar. There is no altar in this place, only a raised platform.

I do not understand these people. Their women do nothing. They listen as one man after another stands up on the platform and speaks, and they clap their hands together with a sound like sails rattling in the wind. They leaf backwards and forwards through the pages of their black books and nod their heads. I do not understand their way of worship. They are from a different time and a different place that has nothing to do with me.

Is it really true that the male god can read the thoughts of my heart? Dare I risk a prayer to the Goddess? I close my eyes and try to feel some connection with their god, but there is nothing. I find I cannot even pray to the Goddess in this place. I look around at the intent faces of the Worshipers, and at the uncomprehending faces of the Risen, and wonder what I am doing here. I stare down at my hands and shudder. They are not *my* hands. When I was a child, I fell and cut my hand on a smashed pot. It left three white scars on the fleshy pad below my thumb. There are no scars now.

I did not remember when I was first awakened, what was the manner of my death. Now I recall it – how we died. The sea rose up over us and we perished. The waters had given us life. They had provided us with all the food we needed in abundance. We had lived well and the Goddess loved us. We were happy. In the end, the sea that gave us birth reclaimed us. Surely, that is as it should be.

The woman, the stranger, tells me what this meeting is about. She says that the Risen are not approved by the male god, Jehovah, like the other Worshipers are, because in our past lives we did not worship him. We have been raised up to learn about him and to be judged by him at the end of many years. She does not say what will happen after that.

I feel my face burning at the insult and the indignity of our position.

There was a fat woman in our village who always smiled and seemed agreeable, but however many fish we caught in our nets, she boasted that her husband had caught more, her sons were stronger and more handsome, her daughters more beautiful, and her house more ornately adorned than any other person in the village. When she said those things, she had that same expression on her face as the woman, the stranger, has now.

I am filled with dread. I did not ask to be raised up from the sleep of the dead. I am angered that my Goddess should be swept aside as if she never existed; outraged that this demanding god, whom we never knew, expects us to fall down and worship him under threat of judgement. What is this but a living death?

Another thought steals into my mind, a small circlet of warmth that surrounds my anguished heart and makes it beat faster.

Asikira.

I do not even know if our village still exists. Perhaps it lies, long buried, beneath the waters, but my husband and sons may be there, or nearby. Suddenly I know I must try to find it. When I get back to the tenement block, I will ask the woman, the stranger. I realize that I do not like her very much, but she is the only one who may know. Maybe she can take me there. What have I got to lose?

I should not have asked. She said she did not know the place. She shook her head and told me it was a bad idea. I did not like the look in her eyes. She remarked that I am unusual because most of the Risen do not have such a clear memory of their past lives. I shrugged and tried to look as if it were unimportant.

I am determined to search for Asikira on my own. I am in a state of high anxiety. I must be careful that I am not missed, so I plan to set out after dark. The moon is a pale sliver of light just now, so I must wait until there is enough moonlight for me to see my way. The difficulty is that I still do not know exactly where I am. The sea can only be glimpsed between blocks, far in the distance.

It has been agony waiting for the right moment to leave. Finally, there is enough light to travel by tonight. I have a bag prepared with a bottle of water and some dried fruit for my journey. Everyone is asleep now, and I steal down the stair and let myself out through the back entrance. Whatever happens, I am determined never to go back.

Outside, nobody is about. Nothing stirs, but still the faint, acrid smell of burning and an underlying rottenness cling to the air. I glance upwards, wondering if the woman, the stranger, is watching me from her window, but except for the dimly lit stairway, all is in darkness. I set off on the same road we travel to the temple of the male god, but I plan to leave it as soon as possible and find a path that leads directly towards the sea. If I make my way to the coast, I will surely be able to recognize the coastline and take my bearings from there.

The world is silent. Apart from the narrow, cultivated strips surrounding the tenement blocks, there is nothing but scrub. The landscape I knew is stripped away as if it had never existed. The trees that brought us shade from the burning sun have vanished without a trace, not even a stump to mark where they had grown. Crumbled houses lie scattered about like corpses picked clean, gleaming faintly in the moonlight.

I quicken my steps, still searching all around me to make sure I am alone, afraid I might be followed. I am thankful, for once, for my dark clothing and pull its soft hood up over my head.

The road is long and the landscape unrelentingly bleak, but eventually the land begins to dip downwards and I can feel a cool breeze blowing in off the sea. Shreds of ripped clouds float across the moon, but not enough to prevent me from seeing my way. After what seems like an eternity, the road veers off eastwards, but just as I had hoped, there is a dirt path that looks as if it might lead to the coast. Standing next to it is a post with some writing on it, but I have not learned enough to understand what it says.

Tall bushes meet in an arch above my head. I cannot see my feet and I imagine at every step that I might fall into a deep pit. I breathe a sigh of relief when the tunnel opens out again and I observe, with a little lifting of the spirits, that I am much closer to the ocean. I can see it sparkle and glitter, splitting the moonlight into a million silvery jewels. Still, I must be careful. Sometimes after a storm, the edge of the land falls into the sea. Even now, I could find myself suddenly spinning downwards into oblivion.

Ahead of me, hunched against the backdrop of the water, is a low building with a long stone wall enclosing it, a dwelling house almost certainly belonging to one of Jehovah's Worshipers. There is a light inside, and I pray my path does not take me too close to it. I tread as softly as I can, but suddenly the night erupts with the sound of furious barking, and a dog hurls itself at the wall as I pass. I feel sick with panic, start to run, but then throw myself sideways into the bushes. If the owner comes to find out what the commotion is about, I must not be seen. I pray to the Goddess that the dog will not jump the wall and find me. I hear a door open and an angry voice calling. The dog quietens down, but there are footsteps. Then they stop. After an age, in which I can hardly breathe, the

180

footsteps recede again and the door bangs shut. Silence. I wait, but there is no further sound. Slowly I raise myself to my feet and continue my journey, shivering now, my knees gashed, scratches burning down the length of my arms and around my ankles.

The path drops down more steeply. Soon, I can hear the sound of the sea carried inland on the breeze, murmuring, whispering; its soft voice almost unbearably sad. It mourns for me, for my children, my husband. I cannot stop the sudden surge of memories it awakens, and it seems to me that I have no memory that does not include the presence of the sea; its myriad sounds, its angry grey storms, its turquoise calm, its treacherous depths filled with swarming fish and strange sea creatures.

I walk on, lost to the world, until I find myself passing a boat sitting on a wheeled structure. An involuntary cry of excitement escapes my lips. The sea is right here in front of me! I halt, transfixed by its overwhelming presence, so palpable it seems to speak to me. Now it comforts me, tries to soothe my soul and persuade me that I have nothing to fear. Standing at its edge, I close my eyes and listen for a few moments before gathering my resolve.

At first, I think the path has ended, dropping down into the water, but then I see that this is merely a slope to launch boats. The path itself continues around the coast to the west. As I turn aside, something catches my eye.

Pulled up on the slope is another boat, smaller than the first, with a pair of oars resting on the seat inside.

I am a fisherman's daughter. As a child, my father would sometimes allow me to join my brothers, and we would set out to check the lobster pots and explore the coast in our small boat. I was never more proud than when my father let me take a turn at the oars. I proved myself as good as any of my brothers, although they would never admit it.

I look critically at the boat floating on the water. This one is not so different. It seems well kept. Would it not be a safer way of moving along the coast than to follow an uncertain path? Of course, there is a possibility that I will be seen, but I will probably be mistaken for a fisherman checking my lobster pots. Besides, a small boat on a dark ocean in the middle of the night is unlikely to be noticed. I glance around to make sure there is nobody watching, deftly undo the rope that ties the boat, launch it into the water and take up the oars.

Pulling away from the shoreline as rapidly as I can, I soon clear the tiny harbor and find the coastline opening up in front of me. Almost at once the island looks familiar, and yet unfamiliar. I recognize the sweeping black shape of the skyline pressed against the gem-studded sky, its three ridged mountains unmistakeable, but the coastline is not as I remember it. At least, not quite the same as I remember. I move further away from the harbor and a broad, smooth bay spreads out ahead of me. Scattered close to the shore are many low buildings, their distinctive shapes picked out by the light of the moon, like pale gulls' eggs cocooned in nests of dark twigs. These must be the dwelling houses of the Worshipers. I try to make out their surroundings, the cultivated gardens, the lush trees, vibrant fruits, and fragrant blossoms, but it is too dark and too far away to see color or detail.

Close to the shore, I see a fire burning and animated figures moving around it. They are not looking out to sea, but watching the flames. The sound of laughter carries faintly across the water to me, and I can hear the voice of a child calling. Instinctively, I turn my boat to the horizon and move further out to sea, making sure I dip my oars silently. When I turn parallel to the shore again, the figures look like dolls around a flickering candle. The child's voice haunts my mind. I long so much to hear the voices of my sons, their laughter and their songs. Their silence is like a black wall of darkness without end.

My bruised heart gives a sudden leap as a ragged hope flares within it. At the far end of the bay, I recognize a headland shaped like a sea serpent's head, part of its writhing body visible above the sea line. Asikira lies just beyond that headland, I am sure of it! Then I frown. Something about it is not quite right. I know the lie of the land and I know the sea, and the relationship between the two is somehow changed, although I am not certain in what way it has changed.

My arms are tired and my body aching, but I force myself to keep on rowing, pulling, lifting, dipping, towards the sea serpent. A sense of foreboding is settling down on me, threatening to overwhelm me, and rob me of my resolve. *The sea serpent's body has sunk down into the sea.* I was uncertain at first, but I know this headland, and I am sure I am right. Dread creeps into my mind. If the sea serpent is sunk down, then so might be Asikira.

There is no turning back, no alternative but to continue my approach towards the serpent, knowing that around the other side of its gaping jaws lies my village, either above the sea, or drowned beneath it.

The moon is only just above the dark bulk of the mountains as I negotiate the current around the headland. The cave that forms the serpent's yawning mouth is a menacing oval of blackness. I remember with a tingling shiver of horror that as a small child I used to be afraid of passing near it, fearing that a poisonous tongue would come snaking out and strike us, sinking our boat and sending us down into the bottomless deep. My brothers would insist on mooring at the entrance to explore the cave, disappearing into its cavernous jaws, while I huddled in the bottom of the boat with a blanket drawn up around my head.

That child is dead now. Instead, a wraith is passing, a haunted creature more terrible even than the maw of the serpent. I concentrate on steering my boat away from the hissing rush of sea surging inside it. I can hear it booming in the depths of its throat as I pass.

I strain my eyes, expecting to see Asikira at any moment now. In my mind's eye I can see its warm, sun-drenched stone harbor, its fishing fleet arriving with a fresh catch of tuna, its cascade of brightly-painted houses spilling down the hillside, and above its smooth, worn steps, silhouetted on the skyline, the protecting temple of the Goddess. I can feel the beating of my heart; my hands tremble at the oars, every fibre of my body aches and strains with a longing for home.

A crawling horror seeps through my mind, entering into its darkest recesses, seeking out and throttling even the faintest glimmer of hope. No harbor emerges out of the darkness to welcome me. The abandoned houses that rise abruptly out of the sea are nothing but vacant skulls, gleaming and obscene in the waning light of the moon, their roofs collapsed inwards, ravaged interiors exposed to the sky, their doors rotted away, and their walls patched with palsied stains like festering sores.

Wordlessly, I mouth the name of the Goddess, but raising my eyes to the hill above the ruins I see her temple weep, its magnificent façade reduced to nothing more than a few broken pillars. An agonized cry pierces the darkness, echoes off the peeling walls, and repeats itself over and over – an appalling sound - my own voice, unbidden – the voice of my despair bursting from my body.

I wish I had never come here. I wish I had never seen this place, this sunken wreckage more terrible than anything I have yet experienced. I am lost. I am forsaken. I cover my face with my hands. May the waters rise over me! May the Goddess release me!

A sudden sound makes me raise my head quickly. An armed vehicle, like the bulk of a crouching beast is sliding behind the collapsed houses. Another movement. A shadow. Something is approaching along the ruined street, making its way down to the edge of the sea.

A woman. The woman. The stranger. Her face is a death mask. She stands at the water's edge in silence... and watches me.

ORGANIZATION

"Guilt is never a rational thing; it distorts all the faculties of the human mind, it perverts them, it leaves a man no longer in the free use of his reason, it puts him into confusion." – Edmund Burke, 1729

Tracts

Millie was helping her mother distribute tracts. She had collected a pile of them from the hall table to put in her satchel. Now she was handing them out along the street, door to door, as quickly as she could. Biting cold nipped at her fingers through her woollen gloves and her feet seemed to soak up the cold as she stood on each doorstep, explaining briefly what the tracts were about. Sometimes people just closed the door again without taking one, or else snatched one quickly out of her hands before going back inside to the warmth of their hearths.

On the front of the tract was a picture of a man sweeping some corpulent-looking gentlemen off the globe of the earth. This picture, her mother had explained, was an illustration of how the New Order would sweep away wicked, greedy men and cleanse the earth of hostile societies. Only then would Utopia be realised. It was imminent, her mother told her. Close at hand. All they had to do was be loyal, obedient and submissive, and soon they would see it all taking place.

187

Millie had been told all these things many times, but she still did not really understand. How could whole societies be swept away like that? There one day – gone the next. She would much rather play with her friends. It was Saturday, and she knew many of the girls in her class at school would be going ice-skating. If she pleaded hard enough, maybe her mother would let her go, but deep down, she already knew what her mother's response would be.

Predictably, it went just as she had feared. Her mother spoke about "commitment" and "responsibility" with that obstinate look on her face that Millie knew so well. With a heavy sigh of resignation, she prepared herself mentally for a dull morning.

***

Well over seven million Jehovah's Witnesses are active worldwide, but what is remarkable about these scattered groups is that in every country in which they operate, there is total compliance with *Watchtower* doctrines. Unquestioning obedience and uncritical acceptance in the face of multiple changes in doctrine and failure of prophecies is a distinctive feature of their culture. There is not a nation on earth that can boast the same level of control that the Watchtower Bible and Tract Society (WTBTS) has over its subjects. How is this possible? How has the Organization of Jehovah's Witnesses succeeded in gaining such rigid control over the hearts and minds of its members?

Lying at the heart of the culture is a unique mechanism that ensures total obedience to the dictates of the Governing Body; the policy of shunning. This policy guarantees the ability to cut off any individual from his or her entire family and friends, almost instantaneously. In order to understand how the shunning policy grants the Governing Body this level of control, it is necessary to understand more about the Organization and how it operates.

First of all, the Governing Body is the central hub of the entire Organization of Jehovah's Witnesses. It is separate and distinct from the Watchtower Bible and Tract Society, which is merely the legal organization used by them to coordinate its operations worldwide and to facilitate the work of publishing its many books, pamphlets, leaflets, and magazines. At the time of writing, the WTBTS has its headquarters in Brooklyn, New York, and there are branches worldwide.

Currently, the Governing Body itself also operates out of Brooklyn, New York. It comprises of just eight members who occupy a unique position within the Organization of Jehovah's Witnesses. Unlike a democratic system, which elects members to government office, the Governing Body appoints itself without reference to rank and file. Reinforcing a top-down approach, the Governing Body claims that there are two classes of people.

First and foremost are 144,000 "anointed" Christians – an elite class who will rule as priests and kings with Christ in his heavenly kingdom for a thousand years after Armageddon. (Revelation 14:1-4) Those claiming to be anointed by God as prospective members of the 144,000 make up a 'remnant' of spiritually 'anointed' people on earth, who believe they will be 'changed' or resurrected to rule with Christ in his heavenly kingdom at God's appointed time. The Governing Body at Brooklyn represents about 12,000 dedicated Witnesses around the world who also profess to be anointed followers of Christ.

Prior to October 2012, *all* the "anointed" members still living were believed to comprise God's "faithful and discreet slave" class on earth, as identified in Matthew 24:45.

"Who really is the faithful and discreet slave whom his master appointed over his domestics, to give them their food at the proper time?"

In this capacity, the "faithful and discreet slave" class took on the task of interpreting God's will as written in the Bible and provided spiritual "food" to the "domestics" or non-anointed members of the Christian congregations by means of public talks, books, and magazine articles, etc. The Governing Body was obliged to consult with all other members of the "faithful and discreet slave" class on matters of policy or changes in doctrine. However, the announcement at an annual general meeting held at Jersey Assembly Hall, New Jersey, on 6th October 2012 revealed "new light" concerning the identity of the "faithful and discreet slave." In short, the Governing Body at Brooklyn, Bethel now claims to be the "faithful and discreet slave" in its entirety, operating as such in their decision-making capacity and when preparing articles for publication. The rest of the 'anointed' members still living, are no longer considered members of the 'faithful and discreet slave' class and, in future, will not be consulted by the Governing Body.

The great crowd

As for the subordinate, second class of people, most of the congregation of Jehovah's Witnesses is made up of those who expect a resurrection to life on earth under the rulership of the kingdom of Christ. (Revelation 7:9; John 10:16) The distinctive feature separating these from the "anointed" is the claim that the Bible addresses itself only to the "anointed" class. Members who profess to have an "earthly hope", rather than a "heavenly" one, are taught that they can only access the Bible through the "faithful and discreet slave" on earth, i.e. the Governing Body.

All congregations of Jehovah's Witnesses are led to believe that the Bible cannot be read and understood without spiritual insight and necessary guidance from the appointed "faithful and discreet slave" class. (Matthew

191

24:42-46) Without them, the rank and file believe that they cannot discover the "deep things of God." The Bible must be interpreted for them, its light revealed and dispensed by "the faithful and discreet slave." (1 Corinthians 2:10; Proverbs 3:5,6)

"All who want to understand the Bible should appreciate that the 'greatly diversified wisdom of God' can become known only through Jehovah's channel of communication, the faithful and discreet slave." *The Watchtower*, 1 October, 1994, page 8

Governing Body appointed for life

The Governing Body of Jehovah's Witnesses is responsible for formulating all policy and guidance on spiritual and doctrinal matters, and for producing much of the material found in *The Watchtower* and *Awake!* magazines, and other publications of Jehovah's Witnesses.

In democratic countries, leaders of government and the business world accept that it is in the best interests of their country or business to limit the terms of their own power. They recognize that safeguards, checks, and balances must be put in place because humans tend to lose their grip on reality when they are given access to unlimited power and authority without time limit. The historical record is filled with colorful examples to illustrate that the human mind cannot cope with an extended period of absolute power. Roman Emperors from Caligula to Commodus, religious leaders from the Borgias to cult leader, Jim Jones, and dictators from Stalin, Pol Pot, and Iddi Amin to Saddam Hussein and Muammar Qaddafi, given unlimited power and authority, follow the same pattern; they eliminate all opposition and surround themselves exclusively with submissive supporters. Eventually, they lose all sense of reality and believe themselves to be infallible.

It is disturbing, then, that the Governing Body of Jehovah's Witnesses has appointed itself, with absolute power, for life. Eight men have uncontested control over millions of people worldwide – people who have not elected them to office and who are denied the right to challenge any of their decisions.

If you were to ask any one of Jehovah's Witnesses, "Who do you serve? Who do you obediently follow?" they will always answer that they obey their God, Jehovah under the direction of his son, Jesus Christ. If their belief in Jehovah, Jesus Christ, or the Bible is criticized, Jehovah's Witnesses usually remain calm as they seek to refute the argument. However, if the Governing Body is criticized, they become agitated, distressed, offended, and even angry. Why?

In practice, every instruction and every decision made by the Governing Body of Jehovah's Witnesses is accepted and scrupulously observed without question. Challenging a biblical interpretation or querying a Governing Body decision would be considered evidence of disrespect for

God's arrangement and, therefore, would be tantamount to opposing God himself. It begs the question, are Jehovah's Witnesses really followers of their God Jehovah and Jesus Christ, or followers of the Governing Body?

While claiming that it is not infallible, still the reality is that the "faithful and discreet slave" or Governing Body is accorded a reverence greater than many Catholics give to the Pope. (Matthew 24:45,46) In Catholic society, it is well known that a large percentage of members ignore the Pope's instructions on contraception. Such widespread disobedience would be unimaginable within the Jehovah's Witnesses society. Whatever the Governing Body has to say is regarded as coming directly from God himself. Biblical interpretations are uncritically accepted, unanimously, as inspired by God.

> "Publications that help us to understand the Bible are provided by 'the faithful and discreet slave.' These make available a wealth of information concerning vital spiritual matters. (Matt. 24:45; 1 Cor. 2:12, 13) ...they focus on how to serve God acceptably and gain his approval. Such wholesome reading will help you to develop as a spiritual person." [69]

Again,

> "Through 'the faithful and discreet slave,' Jehovah has also provided the timely journals, *The Watchtower* and *Awake!* and other Bible-based publications. (Matthew

24:45) Diligently studying these will fortify us spiritually. Yes, we must take the time – 'buy out the opportune time' – for personal study." *The Watchtower*, 1 October, 1999, page 18

This top-down structure is similar to Christendom's clergy-laity distinction so disdained by the Witnesses, but it exercises far more control over their daily lives than is generally the case in Christendom. It is responsible for ensuring that ordinary members of Jehovah's Witnesses remain obedient to the Governing Body and accept whatever it teaches them, without question.

Elders and ministerial servants

The appointment of ministerial servants and elders within the congregation is handled by local congregational elders. Ministerial servants must be dedicated, baptized members of the congregation. They must demonstrate their suitability by attendance at all meetings, regular participation in 'field service' (knocking on doors), and in exemplary behavior. Ministerial servants handle clerical and attendant duties, handle congregational accounts, and act as literature coordinators.

The qualifications for appointment as an elder are similar to those for a ministerial servant. In addition, those seeking appointment as elders must be mature adults, capable of overseeing the congregation, and presiding over its meetings. Elders take part in pastoral work, direct the preaching work, and organize and take part in judicial committees to deal with members suspected of breaching the Governing Body's directives. They are advised to consult Paul's letter to Timothy, in which it is explained that those "taking the lead" should be,

> "...irreprehensible, a husband of one wife, moderate in habits, sound in mind, orderly, hospitable, qualified to teach, not a drunken brawler, not a smiter, but reasonable, not belligerent, not a lover of money, a man presiding over his own household in a fine manner, having children in subjection with all seriousness; (if indeed any man does not know how to preside over his own household, how will he take care of God's congregation?) not a newly converted man, for fear that he might get puffed up [with pride] and fall into the judgment passed upon the Devil. Moreover, he should also have a fine testimony from people on the outside, in order that he might not fall into reproach and a snare of the Devil." 1 Timothy 3:2-7

No secular educational requirements are necessary, and women are excluded from all such appointments. Once the decision is made, and an individual appears to meet the requirements, a recommendation is made by the existing congregational elders to the Governing Body of Jehovah's Witnesses.

Children and education

Children of Jehovah's Witnesses are raised in their parents' religion and expected, from infancy, to attend all weekly meetings and accompany their parents on the door-to-door ministry. As they grow, they must participate in family study of *The Watchtower* publications and start taking an active part in speaking to people on the doors, offering them brochures and magazines. At the Kingdom Ministry School,[70] children as young as six years old begin to deliver brief talks to the congregation from the platform.

The Governing Body of Jehovah's Witnesses strongly discourages education beyond that required by law. Any encouragement to seek higher education is viewed as a deceptive lure or a temptation, placed in the same prohibitive class as drugs, or pornography. A *Watchtower* magazine of 1 September, 2008 under the heading, *'What Will Be The End Afterward?'* expresses it this way:

"Young people are often exposed to temptations and pressures to experiment with things that seem popular. Here are some likely scenarios.

Someone dares you to smoke a cigarette.

A well intentioned teacher urges you to pursue higher education at a university.

You are invited to a party where alcohol and possibly drugs will be freely available.

"Why don't you post your profile on the Internet?" someone suggests.

A friend invites you to watch a movie that features violence or immorality.

"If you are ever confronted with any such situations, what will you do? Will you simply give in, or will you carefully consider what the 'end afterward' could be? You would be wise to ask yourself, 'Can a man rake together fire into his bosom and yet his very garments not be burned? Or can a man walk upon the coals and his feet themselves not be scorched?' – Proverbs 6:27,28." [Emphasis mine]

The publications frequently warn against indiscriminate use of the Internet, such as the following notice from page 31 of the brochure, *'Who Are Doing Jehovah's Will Today?'*, headed, "A Note of Caution." Observe the use of loaded language, assumptions, and direct dictate.

"Some Internet sites have been set up by opposers to spread false information about our organization. Their intent is to draw people away from serving Jehovah. We should avoid those sites."

The Governing Body encourages members to believe that the best education can be found within the Organization's own publications.

"Publications that help us to understand the Bible are provided by 'the faithful and discreet slave.' These make available a wealth of information concerning vital spiritual matters. (Matt. 24:45; 1 Cor. 2:12, 13) They also keep us abreast of important world developments and their meaning, help us to become better acquainted with the natural world, and teach us ways to cope with issues that concern us." [71]

Jehovah's Witnesses consider themselves to be rational, thinking people, and celebrate their knowledge of science and history, but only to the extent that the Governing Body approves it. The Governing Body takes upon itself the authority to decide which parts of history and science are acceptable and which are not. No one dares read a book covering a part of science or history that the Governing Body condemns. In these instances, science and history are ridiculed as "worldly wisdom."

> *"For the wisdom of this world is foolishness with God; for it is written: 'He catches the wise in their own cunning.' And again: 'Jehovah knows that the reasonings of the wise men are futile.'"* 1 Corinthians 3:19,20

Those born within the confines of the Organization of Jehovah's Witnesses know little about the outside world, and have been taught how to view it and what attitude to take towards it from information coming from the platform at their Kingdom Halls, and from the Watchtower society's publications. No encouragement is given them to widen out and explore the world at large, or the "wealth of information" contained in publications outside the Organization. As a result, a vast repository of unbiased information and knowledge is closed to them.

Pressure to avoid further education has resulted in successive generations of Jehovah's Witnesses missing out on the pleasure of lifelong learning and the excitement of discovery. Many fail to develop the necessary academic acumen, discipline, or skills necessary to work in anything other than low-paid menial jobs with little responsibility.

Reinforcement by repetition

In order for this situation to exist, much emphasis is placed on the necessity for their congregations to "*all speak in agreement, and that there should not be divisions among you, but that you may be fitly united in the same mind and in the same line of thought.*" (1 Corinthians 1:10). To meet this demand for uniformity, repetitive instruction is necessary, and all books, magazines, and meetings must reiterate the same information.

As an example, Jehovah's Witnesses conduct a weekly '*Watchtower* Study' at their Kingdom Halls, which contains articles of instruction written by members of the Governing Body of Jehovah's Witnesses. The main study article is read aloud from the platform, paragraph by paragraph. For each paragraph, at the bottom of the page there is a set of questions. These questions are put to the audience, but responses *must* coincide with the information given in the paragraph. Members can repeat portions of it, paraphrase it, or give examples to illustrate its veracity. No critical debate is invited. Instead, as many individuals as possible are invited to comment favorably on the paragraphs. In this way, the Governing Body's message or stance is reinforced, reaffirmed, and consolidated by repetition, both individually and as a group.

The same *Watchtower* article is studied in every congregation in every country of the world (where local congregations exist), as far as possible, at the same time. All meetings follow the same pattern of questioning, requiring answers that ensure uniformity of thought and action. With the emphasis on *"all speaking in agreement"* the language of *"the truth,"* there is no room for freedom of expression. (John 8:32; 1 Corinthians 1:10) Publishers of the *"good news"* are taught standard responses to overcome "objections" from outsiders rather than considering them in the light of logic and reasoning. Outsiders' points of view are accepted only as a vehicle in order to introduce the "correct" viewpoint.

Internal language

Every niche group and organization has an internal language understood by its members, but largely unintelligible to those on the outside. Computer programers, bankers and insurers, economists and scientists, even cyclists and train spotters – it seems that wherever humans form themselves into groups for any mutual purpose they develop their own terminology to a greater or lesser extent.

The Watchtower Society is no exception. Individual members are addressed as "brothers" and "sisters" in "the truth." Watchtower Society literature and sermons addressed to their flock contain language not readily understood by a casual observer, for example,

> "faithful and discreet slave" "other sheep" "wicked system of things" "solid food" "leaven" "anointed" "great crowd" "headship" "goats" "antitypical" "ministry" "pre-study" "shepherding call" "subjection;" "mental regulating" "selective foresight" "reaching out" "meat in due season" "new system" "territory" "local need;" "field service" "publisher;" "pioneer" "worldly" "demonized" "field group" "tribulation" "theocratic warfare" "stand up to Hitler" "propitiatory sacrifice" "undeserved kindness" "theocratic arrangement" "Bethelite."

Distinctive language and terminology performs a useful function in terms of precision and accuracy within the context of internal communication, but it can also reinforce the tribal aspect of an Organization, conferring upon its members exclusivity and a feeling of belonging to a unique group of privileged people, privy to information inaccessible to those on the outside.

Monopoly of means of communication

To protect and enhance organizational unity, members are forbidden to consult or purchase secular critical works. These are considered 'apostate' or corrupt, 'worldly' publications. If discovered reading such material, members risk being disfellowshipped (see the subheading, 'disfellowshipping and shunning'). Such restrictions, coupled with disincentives to pursue a university education, limit members' access to unbiased information that will enable them to make informed decisions.

Systematic and pervasive control alters the way individual members think, subverting free will and restricting independent thought and critical analysis. Gradually members' self-confidence and self-reliance is undermined. Adherents learn to place implicit trust in "Jehovah's revealed purpose" as it is communicated through the Governing Body, rather than employ their own critical faculties to evaluate the information presented to them and verify the facts, without restrictions on sources of information.

Andrew Holden makes the observation,

> "...the Watch Tower Society controls millions of people who are denied freedom of speech, freedom of the press, freedom of assembly and freedom of conscience yet, paradoxically... devotees regard themselves as free, and non-members as oppressed." [72]

Urgency

Another way in which the Governing Body of Jehovah's Witnesses maintains control over its members is by fomenting a sense of urgency with respect to the preaching work. All are kept in a perpetual state of high alert. *The Watchtower* magazines regularly publish articles such as, 'Keep on the Watch – Why So Important?' (October 15, 2011 study edition); 'Learn Watchfulness from Jesus' Apostles' (January 15, 2012 study edition); and 'Maintain Your Sense of Urgency' (March 15, 2012 study edition). By means of this steady diet of study articles, it is impressed upon members that they are living in the "last days of this wicked system of things." Armageddon is imminent; therefore it is urgent to preach the good news. The preaching work must be accomplished *now*, before the coming destruction by God and the annihilation of all the wicked.

A parallel with George Orwell's classic novel, *1984* is unavoidable. In Oceania, a dystopian government actively seeks to instill in its subjects the notion that the world is in a state of perpetual war, with the objective of unifying its subjects against a common enemy. All-pervasive government surveillance and public mind control is the accepted norm. Its political system is administered by an elite Inner Party, but they, in turn, are subordinate to Big Brother, the deified party leader. Under his authority, individuality is discouraged, and the ability to reason independently is considered a thought crime. The subjects of Oceania subordinate themselves to the collective greater good.

As Holden comments,

"The structure of the [WTBTS] movement and the intense loyalty demanded of each individual at every level demonstrates the characteristics of totalitarianism identified by Friedrich[73]: namely, an elaborate total ideology making chiliastic claims with a promise of a utopian future, a single mass party, a monopoly of the means of communication and central direction and control of activity through bureaucratic co-ordination."

Propaganda

"For it seems to me that God has put us the apostles last on exhibition as men appointed to death, because we have become a theatrical spectacle to the world, and to angels, and to men." 1 Corinthians 4:9

Owing to the Governing Body of Jehovah's Witnesses' complete control of information, they are able to produce a constant stream of propaganda via their publications. In this propaganda, they portray their preaching work as being the most important issue anywhere in the universe. They assert that they are in the forefront of people's minds, that governments all over the world are intensely focussed on them. The Apostle Paul's words above, in his first letter to the congregation in Corinth, are used in support of the idea that everything they do is under intense scrutiny from the world at large and observed with keen interest by heavenly hosts of angels anxious to see the name of their God Jehovah vindicated.

Their insistence that their members must continue to keep themselves separate from the world as much as possible enables them to present the world at large, its morals and its values, as inferior to those within the Organization of Jehovah's Witnesses. (1 Corinthians 6:17) In their literature, Jehovah's Witnesses are portrayed as possessing happiness unimaginable to people in the outside world, who are living in spiritual darkness and are desperately unhappy in a world full of lying, cheating, injustice, and broken homes. Illustrations in Society literature including *The Watchtower* and *Awake!* magazines carry graphic depictions of "worldly" degeneration, for example, rampant crime, domestic violence, defiant children, employees stealing from their employers, and business enterprises steeped in fraudulent activities.

The explicit assumption is that most people on the outside are envious of Jehovah's Witnesses' happy and privileged position, but are unwilling to change their evil ways in order to avail themselves of the opportunity to join their ranks.

In North Korea, the population is given no access to South Korea; therefore its people remain in ignorance of the relative wealth and comfort of people living in the south of the country. North Koreans are therefore easy prey for the propaganda of their Communist party leaders. Jehovah's Witnesses, however, are not set apart physically from the world at large and are free to experience it first-hand, yet they deny the evidence of their own observations.

How is this situation achieved? It can only be accomplished by the Society's rigid insistence on regular meeting attendance at their weekly Public Talk and Watchtower Study, and their Theocratic Ministry School and Service Meeting (which all members must prepare for in advance). These meetings are a powerful means of constant affirmation and reinforcement, both from the platform and by frequent association with fellow members who are taught to believe and speak in total agreement. In this way, it is possible for individual Witnesses to rationalize and minimize the good that they see in the world around them, and to amplify anything bad as confirmation of their beliefs; to recollect negative experiences in the outside world, and to dismiss positive interactions as insubstantial or irrelevant.

The message is hammered home, again and again, that the whole *"world is passing away,"* because it is riddled with corruption and ruled by despotic governments; that Jehovah's only approved Organization is morally superior and that its members are privileged to be subjects of Christ's Kingdom, which is operating via the loving, paternal care of God's appointed servants, the Governing Body. (1 John 2:17)

Marriage, family groups, and children

Jehovah's Witnesses are only permitted to marry within the faith. In practice, this results in large extended family groups of up to forty or fifty people, with perhaps three or four cross marriages within the groups (the younger generation marrying their distant relatives). A typical child will be born into this type of extended family, where all his or her relatives are Jehovah's Witnesses on both the father's and the mother's side. The child will have grandparents, great grandparents, multiple uncles and aunts, and many cousins, nephews, and nieces all in the extended family and all Jehovah's Witnesses.

Since the outside world is depicted as a terrifying place, filled with crime, violence, and unpleasant, wicked people, although the child is allowed to attend school, he or she will be strongly discouraged from making close friends outside the Organization of Jehovah's Witnesses. Extra-curricular activities are not permitted. 'Sleep-overs' and parties with children who are not members of Jehovah's Witnesses are not allowed. It cannot be stressed too strongly that all individuals who are not members of the Organization of Jehovah's Witnesses are regarded as unfit for association, irrespective of their behavior, moral values, or attitude towards them. In their view, individuals are either on God's side, or Satan's side. (Matthew 12:30) There is no middle ground.

It is important to understand that, as a typical 'born-in,' raised within the Organization of Jehovah's Witnesses, every single person they know closely – every one of their friends and all their relatives – will be a member of Jehovah's Witnesses. 'Born-ins', in a sense, are bred in captivity without free access to information, education, choice of friends, or recreation.   As 'born-ins' grow towards adulthood, they too are compelled to limit their selection of potential marriage partners to only those within the Organization.

In this way, Jehovah's Witnesses create a society in which children and young adults are totally dependent on the Organization for their mental well-being. This is what gives the Governing Body its unique control over their membership. They are able to use the extended family as a weapon against any dissenting voice.

Control of family

"No one should be forced to worship in a way that he finds unacceptable or be made to choose between his beliefs and his family." *Awake!* July 2009, page 29

Contrary to the above statement, Jehovah's Witnesses believe that their worship of Jehovah is more important than blood ties, whether they are fellow Witnesses or not. They take to heart the words of Jesus, speaking to his disciples:

"Do not think I came to put peace upon the earth; I came to put, not peace, but a sword. For I came to cause division, with a man against his father, and a daughter against her mother, and a young wife against her mother-in-law. Indeed, a man's enemies will be persons of his own household. He that has greater affection for father or mother than for me is not worthy of me; and he that has greater

affection for son or daughter than for me is not worthy of me." Matthew 10:34-37

Jesus' words, together with those of the Apostle Paul, are invoked as justification for the practice of shunning, the distinctive behavior displayed towards fellow Jehovah's Witnesses, including family members, who have serious doubts about their religion, or about God and the Bible in general.

> "Christians do not hold themselves aloof from people. We have normal contacts with neighbors, workmates, schoolmates, and others, and witness to them even if some are 'fornicators, greedy persons, extortioners, or idolaters.' Paul wrote that we cannot avoid them completely, 'otherwise we would have to get out of the world.' He directed that it was to be different, though, with 'a brother' who lived like that: 'Quit mixing in company with anyone called a brother that [has returned to such ways], not even eating with such a man.'" 1 Corinthians 5:9-11; Mark 2:13-17 [74]

The inference here is that most people outside their Organization are likely to have low moral standards and should be avoided as much as possible. It follows that those who rejoin "worldly" people (people who are not Jehovah's Witnesses) must be avoided and shunned.

Members are encouraged to believe that doubters are motivated by a desire to engage in debauched activities, or guilty of being corrupted by selfish, materialistic "desires

210

of the flesh." If they voice any misgivings on organizational doctrines, they are condemned as apostates.

Fifty to sixty thousand Jehovah's Witnesses are disfellowshipped every year. They are ostracized and shunned by the Organization and all its members. Why is this? *The Watchtower*, April 15, 1988 gives this explanation for the practice of shunning:

> "In the apostle John's writings, we find similar counsel that emphasizes how thoroughly Christians are to avoid such ones: 'Everyone that pushes ahead and does not remain in the teaching of the Christ does not have God... If anyone comes to you and does not bring this teaching, never receive him into your homes or say a greeting to him. For he that says a greeting [Greek, khai'ro] to him is a sharer in his wicked works.'" —2 John 9-11." [75]

Those who leave the Organization understand that if they persist in harboring alternative viewpoints, they risk being considered "mentally diseased," and shunned. Consider this extract taken from *The Independent*, under the heading, 'War of words breaks out among Jehovah's Witnesses,' Tuesday 27th September, 2011.

> "An article published in July's edition of *The Watchtower* warns followers to stay clear of 'false teachers' who are condemned as being 'mentally diseased' apostates who should be avoided at all costs. 'Suppose that a doctor told you to avoid contact with someone who is infected with a

contagious, deadly disease,' the article reads. 'You would know what the doctor means, and you would strictly heed his warning. Well, apostates are "mentally diseased", and they seek to infect others with their disloyal teachings.'"

A copy of the magazine, distributed by Jehovah's Witnesses around the world, was given to *The Independent* by a current member of the church who has become unhappy with official teaching but is afraid to leave for fear of losing his family.

"Many like me remain associated with the Witnesses out of fear of being uncovered as an 'apostate' and ousted, not just from the organization, but from their own friends and families," said the man, who would only give the name John. "I find I am now branded as 'mentally diseased' – giving any who discover my true beliefs free licence to treat me with disdain." [76]

Members of the Organization with serious concerns face the threat of either being disassociated (if they are not a baptized member) or disfellowshipped (if they are baptized).

The threat of being shunned is a successful fear tactic, practically eliminating all potential internal opposition to the organizational message, and preventing many disillusioned people from leaving. Because relationships of any kind outside the congregation are discouraged, if a person leaves – particularly someone who has been born and raised as one of Jehovah's Witnesses – they know they will lose every friend they have ever known, as well as alienate family members who may shun them altogether.

Children and shunning

Even children are not exempt from the punishment of disfellowshipping. The booklet, 'Keep Yourself in God's Love,' 2008 says,

"In some instances, the disfellowshipped family member may still be living in the same home as part of the immediate household... by his course, the individual has chosen to break the spiritual bond between him and his believing family. So loyal family members can no longer have spiritual fellowship with him. For example, if the disfellowshipped one is present, he would not participate when the family gets together to study the Bible. However, *if the disfellowshipped one is a minor child*, the parents are still responsible to instruct and discipline him." (Italics mine)

Disfellowshipped children know that when they leave home they will lose all their friends, and they will be ostracized and shunned by members of their own family. They will be completely alone in a world they have been taught is dangerous, inhospitable, and cruel.

The Watchtower of September 15, 1981, pages 28-9 offers no solace for either parents or their children.

"Sometimes Christian parents have accepted back into the home for a time a disfellowshipped child who has become physically or emotionally ill. But in each case the parents can weigh the individual circumstances. Has a disfellowshipped son lived on his own, and is he now unable to do so? Or does he want to move back primarily because it would be an easier life'? What about his morals and attitude? Will he bring 'leaven' into the home?" – Gal. 5:9

In similar vein, a *Watchtower* study article entitled, 'Let Nothing Distance You From Jehovah', January 2013, gives this advice to parents of a child who has been disfellowshipped:

"Really, what your beloved family member needs to see is your resolute stance to put Jehovah above everything else – including the family bond. So to cope with the situation, be sure to maintain your own spirituality. Do not isolate yourself from your faithful Christian brothers and sisters. (Prov. 18:1) ... Do not look for excuses to associate with a disfellowshipped family member, for example, through e-mail."

Children learn that their parents' love is conditional, and can be snatched away from them instantly if they overstep the demands of their religion.

Shunning – the key to control

"If we stop actively supporting Jehovah's work, then we start following Satan. There is no middle ground." *The Watchtower* 15 July, 2011, page 18

Individuals, whatever their age, who have had a genuine crisis of conscience, or entertain serious doubts about their beliefs, not only suffer the stress of their own inner turmoil, but their situation is painfully exacerbated by the treatment they receive from family members and those whom they have always considered to be their spiritual family. If they were raised within the Organization, that is likely to include a considerable number of people. Former friends, even from childhood, will walk past them in the street without a word. Knowing this will happen as a consequence of their leaving the Organization, many of those who harbor doubts are afraid to voice them, and those who wish to leave because they can no longer accept the religious doctrines, find themselves trapped.

An article compiled by a Humanist Philosophers' group highlights yet another reason for the distress of individuals who find themselves in this situation:

"We each of us want to be able to express our own political and religious and philosophical beliefs, we want to be able to express our deepest feelings and emotions, because these are essential to our sense of who we are. If we have to repress our most personal beliefs and feelings, our very identity is threatened." [77]

Is it any wonder that many former members commonly suffer serious stress-related problems, including anxiety, fear, and disorientation, as well as difficulty reintegrating into society at large?

Many of them have felt the need to seek professional help, while websites offering assistance for ex-Jehovah's Witnesses have sprung up on the Internet. *Jehovah's Witness Recovery*, for instance, claims to offer "to provide an online environment that promotes positive healing and recovery from the Watchtower Society of Jehovah's Witnesses."

It takes an immense effort of will to walk away, fully aware of the punitive treatment that will be meted out. Dependence, guilt, and fear are the driving forces behind more members of Jehovah's Witnesses than anyone will admit. There is no doubt that shunning is a key strategy, the Governing Body's principal means of exerting power and control over its followers.

Another party

While the features I have identified may lead Jehovah's Witnesses to think their organizational arrangement is unique, there is a surprising parallel with a non-religious organization that also emerged early in the twentieth century.

Here are some of its identifying features:

- Belief in a New Order that has not yet arrived
- Importance of keeping on the watch

216

- Propaganda
- Maintaining a state of expectation and urgency
- Declarations of its imminence
- Need for a large number of people to be executed for the benefit of the future happiness of humankind
- Internal 'language' shared by all members
- A belief that all members are equal
- Unquestioning obedience
- Policy of informing on "disloyal" fellow members
- Intolerance of dissenters
- Practice of shunning and disowning family members and relatives.

The story at the beginning of this chapter is not, as may have been supposed, based on a day in the life of a family of Jehovah's Witnesses, but on this other organization. The cover illustration on the brochure they are distributing bears a striking resemblance to Watchtower Bible and Tract Society illustrations of Christ cleansing the earth of wickedness on the Day of Jehovah. In fact, it is based on a 1920s poster depicting Lenin, broom in hand, sweeping royalty and wealthy capitalists off the globe of the Earth, above the caption, "Comrade Lenin cleanses the Earth of Filth."

Basically, the list provided above contains many of the major features of Soviet Communism. Communist ideology, organizational structure, and policy is in many ways remarkably similar to that of the Organization of Jehovah's Witnesses.

Belief in a New Order that has not yet arrived

Vladimir Lenin (1870-1924), inspired by the writings of Karl Marx (originator of the *Communist Manifesto*), adapted the communist ideal for a largely non-industrialized Russia. Lenin and his followers believed in nothing short of a New World Order; the ultimate aim of communism was world revolution and the realization of Utopia worldwide.

In 1919, referring to the First World War, Lenin announced,

> "The war has shown that capitalism is finished and a new order is ready to take its place...Those who are faithful to the cause of liberation from the yoke of capitalism are known by the glorious name of Communists! Soon we shall see the triumph of Communism throughout the whole world!" [78]

The Russian Revolution paved the way for Lenin to establish himself in power in 1917. He changed the name of the Bolshevik section of the Russian Social Democratic Labour Party to the Communist Party of Russia. Swiftly, the communists organized a second revolution that completely overwhelmed the new infant republic and Lenin found himself dictator of Russia. However, his success was considered only one stage on the path to the full establishment of communism. It would take a violent overthrow of capitalism to bring it about completely, and communists were prepared for a large number of people to be executed for the benefit of the future happiness of the rest of humankind.

"Thus the mass-murder program of Communism is a logical and inescapable consequence of their basic beliefs." [79]

The 1920s poster, "Comrade Lenin Cleanses the Earth of Filth," was designed to illustrate their intentions.

Maintaining a state of expectation and urgency

A state of constant expectation and vigilance continued long after Lenin's death in 1924, and warnings against complaisance were issued.

"There is a danger that certain of our comrades, having become intoxicated with success, will get swollen heads and begin to lull themselves with boastful songs, thinking that victory is easy and all threats have been overcome. There is nothing more dangerous than sentiments of this kind, for they weaken the party and disarm its ranks... We must not lull the party, but sharpen its vigilance; we must not sing it to sleep, but sharpen it for action; not disarm it, but arm it; not demobilise it, but keep it in a state of constant readiness..." [80]

Declarations of imminence

Three decades later, the New Order was still considered a future goal. In 1961, Russian Premier Kruschev promised that the building of communism would be completed in the Soviet Union by 1980. The third new Communist Party Program set out the timetable, which promised that, "In the course of the 1970s, housing, public transport, water, gas, and heating will become rent-free for all citizens," concluding with the slogan: "The party solemnly declares that today's generation of Soviet people will live under Communism!" [81]

Internal 'language' shared by all members

The communist movement existed in many countries around the world. Some parties were legal and some illegal. In some countries they formed the biggest party and in others they existed as small minorities. Nevertheless, in all these different countries they used the same language of communism.

Words such as "commitment," "hostile societies," and "the realized Utopia" were common, and the movement's use of language in the media was particularly distinctive. In fact, a team of linguists at Charles University in Prague, headed by Professor František Čermák, has made it their area of study, culminating in 2010, with the publication of *The Dictionary of Communist Totalitarianism*.[82]

Official magazines

Additionally, the communists distributed their own magazines, the foremost in Russia being *Pravda* ('The Truth'), which became an official publication of the Soviet Communist Party in 1918, and was used as a conduit for announcing official policy and policy changes. All citizens were expected to read it. In fact, subscription to *Pravda* was mandatory for state-run companies, the armed services, and other organizations.

Use of family terminology

All members of the communist party were referred to as a brother or 'comrade,' in order to emphasize the importance of their relationship to one another as members of the party. The communist 'family' took precedence over all other relationships.

Party promises

The principles of redistribution of wealth, state-owned means of production, and distribution of equal shares of the benefits derived from labor were sacrosanct.

Oliver Fritz, who lived and worked in communist East Germany, explains,

"The idealistic youth saw communism as the answer to all questions – a world of social justice freed from war and misery, a new and fairer society in which exploitation and money had both been abolished. Service before self for everyone." [83]

Unquestioning obedience and intolerance of dissenters

In his book, *Russia: A 1,000-year Chronicle of the Wild East*, BBC Moscow correspondent, Martin Sixsmith explains,

"Just as Christian Russia believed for centuries that it had a God-given mission to bring truth and enlightenment to mankind, so Russian Communism believed in its own holy destiny to change, educate and perfect the human species. The party would lead us from the grim, corrupted present to the cleansed, harmonious future. But in return it demanded unquestioning obedience from its followers: any deviation or dissent would be mercilessly punished." p.250

Members publicizing political ideas and theories that differed in any way from the Communist Party's official standpoint faced serious disciplinary action.

Policy of informing

Fritz comments,

"Naturally everyone had friends, colleagues, neighbours or acquaintances who they might suspect of collaborating with the Stasi [Ministry of State Security]... Yet the real spies were often the people you trusted most." p.54

Practice of shunning and disowning family members and relatives

In the year 1932, a thirteen-year-old Russian boy denounced his father for "falling under the influence of *kulak* [peasant farmer] relations." Denouncements like this were becoming an increasingly common phenomenon, with newspaper small ads carrying proclamations such as,

"I denounce my sister," or "I break off relations with my mother." But what was significant about this particular denouncement was the fact that this boy became a celebrity. His father was condemned to ten years in a labor camp, where he was eventually shot, yet this boy was elevated to the position of a hero because of his "selflessness."

After his father had been sent away, the boy, Pavlik Morozov, was murdered. According to the official verdict, his uncle and grandfather committed the crime for revenge. They were both given the death penalty, while praise was heaped upon the boy. Maxim Gorky, Soviet author and political activist, remarked that by "overcoming blood kinship, he discovered spiritual kinship." [84]

Sixsmith observes,

> "In a remarkable reversal of natural morality, the state proclaimed that loyalty to family must take second place to loyalty to the ideals of the state." (p.310)

Critics of the regime were often expelled and even declared insane. It was assumed that if anybody opposed the organization destined to usher in happiness to all mankind, he or she must be mad.

Roots

Similarities between the methodology used by the Governing Body to manipulate Jehovah's Witnesses and those used to establish and expand communism in the same time period call into question the claim of divine oversight in the case of the former. Instead, it can be seen that the strategies employed in both cases stem from the same basic root assumptions, motivations, and moral values prevalent at the time.

Communism, while claiming to be godless, deified Lenin. His body was embalmed after his death, and still lies in state for pilgrims to visit. Millions have been spent on preserving it for posterity. Pictures of communist leaders became icons; defacing their images was considered a serious crime, and the writings of Lenin and Marx became the equivalent of holy books.

The deification, power, and authority given to only one individual resulted in persecution, purges, and genocide – just what we see in the Bible's record. Communism is a perfect example of what happens when a state religion holds sway. Its subjects are deprived of their basic freedoms, science and learning are suppressed, and ordinary citizens are mistreated and abused, even put to death for any weakness or perceived lack of loyalty.

Although the Russian totalitarian state is a thing of the past, there are still a few anachronistic, totalitarian states surviving into the twenty-first century, including North

Korea (population 23 million) and the Organization of Jehovah's Witnesses (population 7 million). The former may be beyond our control, but the latter could be resolved by thoughtful regulation in western societies.

**North Korea –the other 21ˢᵗ century totalitarian state
Source: www.flickr.com. John Pavelka, Oct. 2010**

As it stands, the organizational arrangement of Jehovah's Witnesses with its central Governing Body is a top-down arrangement, claiming exclusive authority, whose administrative functions and field of operations are completely outside the control of its members. The rank and file have only the vaguest idea of how it operates. An aura of esoteric wisdom surrounds it, fomented by such statements as,

"Only this organization functions for Jehovah's purpose and to his praise. To it alone God's Sacred Word, the

225

Bible, is not a sealed book" – *The Watchtower*, July 1, 1973, page 402

The organizational ideal, like the communist ideal, allows those in authority to behave as a body in a manner that the individuals involved may find personally objectionable. It allows their consciences to be subsumed in the interests of that ideal, enabling them to act in ways that are insensitive, inhumane, and immoral.

MORALITY REVISITED

Baptism

Ten thousand people listen in rapt attention, straining to hear the words of a figure standing on a rostrum erected in the center of the pitch. Loudspeakers placed at intervals around the stadium dispense his words to the faithful. Ten thousand hands sift softly back and forth through the Holy Scriptures following the sacred passages, the gentle rustle of pages like the hissing of reeds in the wind. Gusts of chill wind sweep across the open space and swirl around the seated figures. They hug their bodies and pull their shawls and blankets more closely around themselves.

Three companions huddle together on the hard seats; a dark-skinned boy of perhaps fourteen, and his companion, a fair-haired boy of fifteen. Next to the fair-haired boy sits a girl, the sister of the dark-skinned boy. She shivers. The fair boy takes off his jacket and places it gently across her shoulders. She turns her head. Jade eyes fringed with ebony lashes smile up at him. A dimple appears in her cheek. The boy gazes down at her in silence.

The sermon continues. The young people appear to take notes of the weighty words delivered from the platform, but in the fair boy's notebook are the words, "I love you," and a name elaborately decorated. The olive-skinned girl glances at the book then lowers her eyes. The two boys talk briefly in low voices, then the fair one turns

227

to the girl and speaks softly to her, his slim hands plaiting the silken threads of her hair. She turns her head away, her face an oval of ecstasy. He whispers something, his lips brushing her cheek. She glances at her mother sitting a few seats away before raising her eyes to his. As the faithful break into applause, she breathes his name.

There is an air of hushed expectation. Another speaker has taken to the rostrum to announce a list of names. The air grows still. The fair boy, raising his head, turns pale. He stands up and the girl gives a shuddering sigh. Slowly she pulls the jacket from her narrow shoulders. Their hands meet as she passes it to him. Wind-whipped fronds of hair conceal her face. He steps back, turns, and is gone.

The girl and her companion sit in motionless silence as they watch the fair-haired boy join the figures on the rostrum. A sharp wind cuts through the words of the announcement; disjointed threads dispersing themselves around the open arena, crackling, incoherent, through the loudspeakers. There is a final burst of applause.

Ten thousand people stand, their voices raised in song, its strength dissipating in the wind as the figures on the rostrum file away to a place of baptism. The girl and her companion, joined by their mother, merge with ten thousand people flowing through the exit, intent on watching the spectacle.

***

228

As we have discovered, Jehovah's Witnesses spend an enormous amount of time feeding their minds on biblical morality. Given its sometimes violent and debased nature, it is of interest to explore what effect such assiduous study has on their own moral values.

Definition

What is morality? The word morality is derived from Latin, *moralis,* meaning custom, or manner. Morality is usually understood with reference to a code of conduct put forward by society, or by religious or other groups, which establishes standards of right and wrong, good and bad behavior that all members agree to abide by, and against which they will be measured. Not everyone would agree on all issues of morality, but there are some general principles that are held in common, for instance, that it is wrong to murder, steal, cheat, or lie. Such acts fall outside what is acceptable, and are therefore considered immoral.

As discussed previously, Jehovah's Witnesses adhere to strict biblical codes of conduct that they consider moral. They place fornication, adultery, and homosexuality high on their list of immoral acts, punishable by disfellowshipping, but their emphasis on the avoidance of "unclean" sexual behavior outside (and even inside) marriage tends to feed into their perception that they are the most moral group of people on earth.

Marriage and morality

The average age at which women and men get married
has been rising steadily in recent years. In the United
States, the average age at first marriage is now 28.7 for
men and 26.5 for women. In the United Kingdom, the
average age for first marriages for women was 23.1 in
1981, climbing to 30 years old for the first time in 2009.
The latest available UK National Statistics figures,
published by the Office for National Statistics, show that
the average age for women marrying in 2010 had risen
again to 33.6 years.

Young people are delaying marriage for a number of
reasons, including the fact that a greater proportion of
women concentrate on educating themselves at university
and establishing a career first. The changing role of
women in society and recognition of the importance of
education and training in determining life prospects has
increased awareness that early marriage is unwise.[85] The
ONS (Office for National Statistics) 2010 survey reports
that the only age group that saw a decrease in the number
of marriages were men and women under twenty years of
age. How do young Jehovah's Witnesses compare?

Witness parents are adamant that their teenage children
should not indulge in any form of sexual activity before
marriage, including heavy petting, sexual intercourse or
masturbation. Even moderate physical demonstrations of
affection are frowned upon on the grounds that they may

lead to more intimacy. Teenagers are advised to make use of chaperones to make sure they don't succumb to any "unclean behavior." Jehovah's Witnesses ignore the fact that these demands bring extreme pressure to bear on young people at a time when their sexual impulses are very strong.

As Naomi Seiler, Associate Research Professor at George Washington University School of Public Health and Health Services suggests,

> "...abstinence-unless-married education, which contends that sex outside of marriage is unhealthy, may have the unintended consequence of encouraging teens to marry before they are ready." [86]

Such is the case with Jehovah's Witnesses. Rigid insistence on the application of biblical strictures, which emphasize the sinfulness of non-marital sex, far from strengthening their resolve, effectively pushes frustrated youths into early marriage as the only acceptable culmination of a romantic relationship.

A number of questions must be borne in mind when considering early marriage.

- Is making a lifelong commitment at the age of seventeen or eighteen the best way to start life?
- Is teen pregnancy desirable, even inside marriage?

- Wouldn't young people be better served if they were encouraged to pursue an education and allowed the time for personal development?
- Is it moral for a society to pressure their teenage children into premature marriage, pregnancy, and childbirth?

Jehovah's Witnesses fail to confront questions like these, or face the fact that teenage rebelliousness, unhappy marriages, and separations are often fruits of the culture *within* their Organization.

Missing altogether, is the understanding that a moral lifestyle encompasses a far broader spectrum of issues than just sexual behavior – that children's rights, women's rights, freedom of religion, behaviour towards family members, the right to education, the death penalty, law, and justice are all essentially moral issues.

Children's rights

Child abuse

To their credit, many young Witness children are good students and respectful toward their teachers. However, since parents view any contact with the outside world as bad, these children are strongly discouraged from making friends at school, participating in extracurricular school activities such as swimming, football, gymnastics, squash, and other sports, or joining a choir, dance, or amateur

232

dramatic society, and of course, associating with schoolmates after school hours. In addition, children are not allowed to involve themselves in any non-Witness social gatherings or political or humanitarian activities, either generally or those sponsored by the school.

Since Jehovah's Witnesses celebrate only weddings, funerals, and the memorial of Christ's death, all other festivities celebrated by the world at large – Thanksgiving, Christmas, New Year, Hallowe'en, birthdays, Bonfire night, and so on – are out of bounds for Witness children and they are forbidden from accepting any well-meant festive gifts from "worldly" schoolmates or relatives. Instead, they are expected to "witness" to the gift-giver concerning the Day and the New Order.

Disobedience to parents is not tolerated. As mentioned earlier, Jehovah's Witnesses follow this biblical advice when disciplining their children:

"Do not hold back discipline from the mere boy. In case you beat him with the rod, he will not die. With the rod you yourself should beat him, that you may deliver his very soul from She'ol itself." Proverbs 23:13-14

In contrast, spanking or smacking a child is condemned as an act of violence and prohibited in an increasing number of countries around the world. As at July 2012, in the

following thirty-three countries children are fully
protected by law from all corporal punishment: [87]

South Sudan (2011)	Albania (2010)	Congo, Republic of (2010)
Kenya (2010)	Tunisia (2010)	Poland (2010)
Liechtenstein (2008)	Luxembourg (2008)	Republic of Moldova (2008)
Costa Rica (2008)	Togo (2007)	Spain (2007)
Venezuela (2007)	Uruguay (2007)	Portugal (2007)
New Zealand (2007)	Netherlands (2007)	Greece (2006)
Hungary (2005)	Romania (2004)	Ukraine (2004)
Iceland (2003)	Germany (2000)	Israel (2000)
Bulgaria (2000)	Croatia (1999)	Latvia (1998)
Denmark (1997)	Cyprus (1994)	Austria (1989)
Norway (1987)	Finland (1983)	Sweden (1979)

A monitoring body for the United Nations Convention on
the Rights of the Child adopted the following comment in
June 2006:

"Addressing the widespread acceptance or tolerance of corporal punishment of children, and eliminating it, in the family, schools and other settings, is not only an obligation of States parties under the Convention. It is also a key strategy for reducing and preventing all forms of violence in societies... Once visible, it is clear that the practice [of corporal punishment] directly conflicts with the equal and inalienable rights of children to respect for their human dignity and physical integrity. The distinct nature of children, their initial dependent and developmental state, their unique human potential, as well as their vulnerability all demand the need for more, rather than less legal and other protection from all forms of violence." [88]

Even in countries that have not prohibited spanking, there is still a decrease in physical punishment. Referring to corporal punishment, Darshak Sanghavi, Chief of Pediatric Cardiology and Associate Professor of Pediatrics at the University of Massachusetts Medical School comments,

"There has been a dramatic reduction in its use over the past two generations—an unprecedented change in a pattern that likely had been fixed for millennia. In the United States, for example, 94 percent of parents endorsed hitting kids in 1968, but only one-half approved by 1999. Similar decreases occurred in countries as diverse as Austria, Sweden, Kuwait, Germany, and New Zealand." [89]

Sanghavi points out that some sociologists, like Murray Straus at the University of New Hampshire, USA, believe the decrease in corporal punishment is part of the civilizing process of society, in which all forms of violence have declined over the last centuries.

In those countries where children are under protection of the secular law, Jehovah's Witnesses often deny that they follow the scriptural injunction at Proverbs 23:13-14 literally.   They refer to the 'rod' as the exercise of discipline and correction, but the New Living Translation of Proverbs 23 gives this rendering of the scripture.

"Don't fail to correct your children. They won't die if you spank them. Physical discipline may well save them from death."   Proverbs 23: 13-14 (New Living Translation)

Jehovah's Witnesses are convinced that the Bible's moral stance on child discipline is superior to that of the protective laws ushered in by secular law. Anecdotal evidence suggests that physical punishment of children by Witness parents is still widely practiced.[90]

Child abuse: Baptism of juveniles

Every year, children of twelve years old and even younger continue to be accepted for baptism, thus dedicating their entire lives to the service of their God, Jehovah.[91] This is a serious commitment, involving the taking of vows.

236

Baptism thus places them in a vulnerable position, because as baptized members of the congregation, they are now expected to behave as adults. From baptism onwards, they are considered wholly accountable for their actions, and may face shunning or disfellowshipping should they be found guilty of any infringement.

Why would such young children put themselves forward for such a serious commitment? One reason could well be the relentless pressure placed upon them from within the Organization of Jehovah's Witnesses.

Below is an extract from a notebook for children (which they were able to download from the Internet), prepared for the 2010 annual convention. Headed, 'Baptism Talk Notes,' it directs these questions to the child:

When do you want to be baptized?
What prevents you from getting baptized?
Why do you want to remain close to Jehovah?
How long do you want to remain close to him?
Have you made a dedication to Jehovah yet?
Are you happy for the people who are being baptized today?
Who is the oldest?
Who is the youngest?
How many were baptized?
Were there mostly boys or girls?
Do you know any of them?

Is it any wonder that children feel pressured to make a dedication? The above page of questions is accompanied by an illustration of Philip and the Ethiopian Eunuch passing a body of water, evoking Acts 8:27-39 in which the Eunuch declares, *"Look! A body of water; what prevents me from getting baptized?"* (verse 36).

If you have read the full account in Acts, you will know that the Ethiopian Eunuch, declaring his eagerness for baptism, was *"a man in power under Candace queen of the Ethiopians, and who was over all her treasure."* This was a powerful, mature man, not a child. Even Jesus himself did not get baptized until he was thirty years old.

Is it responsible behavior on the part of congregational elders to accept the dedication and baptism of people of such tender years?

Child abuse: Sexual abuse

Another pressing problem hidden from the view of prospective members is that pedophiles, who are baptized Witnesses, operate within the Organization. If cases of child abuse are brought to their attention, the internal judicial system ensures that in many cases these offenses are not even reported to the relevant authorities. No professional help is sought when dealing with pedophiles, and scant attention is paid to the victims of their crimes. Pedophiles are forgiven and reinstated at the whim of a body of men (the elders) with no relevant qualifications to deal with this kind of offense, and there is no organized program of rehabilitation for either the offender or the victim.

Nevertheless, many cases of child abuse have come to light in recent years, garnering notoriety in the public press. The most recent scandal in 2012 involved Candace Conti, molested repeatedly when she was nine and ten years old by a member of the North Fremont congregation of Jehovah's Witnesses in California. Conti was awarded $28 million in damages in a landmark ruling; the largest ever jury verdict for a single victim in a religious child abuse case.

The court upheld Conti's claim that the Watchtower Bible and Tract Society of New York adopted a policy in 1989 that instructed congregation elders to keep child abuse allegations secret. When Conti's abuser from the 1990s, Jonathan Kendrick, was convicted in 2004 of molesting another girl, Conti realized that the elders at the North Fremont Congregation of Jehovah's Witnesses had done nothing to prevent him coming into contact with other minors in the congregation.

The court ordered Kendrick to pay sixty percent of the $7 million compensatory damages, while the Watchtower Society was to cover the remaining forty percent of the compensatory damages and all of the $21 million punitive damages. Unfortunately, instead of admitting their culpability and taking steps to safeguard vulnerable children within their Organization, the WTBTS deny any responsibility for what happened to Conti. Instead, at the time of writing they are contesting the decision of the court in an effort to salvage their damaged reputation.

When the scandal of child abuse erupted in the Roman Catholic Church, Jehovah's Witnesses were quick to point an accusatory finger and count it as proof of corruption within the ranks of the Church. Now that the same thing has been exposed within their own ranks, they are denying that there is any corruption on their part.

In many countries, including Northern Ireland, Australia, Canada and the United States, it is mandatory to report a suspected case of child abuse immediately to the police, not to any internal legal system belonging to the organization involved. By not reporting suspected cases of child abuse to the police, Jehovah's Witnesses are breaking the law of the land, as well as God's law as set out in Romans 13:1-7.

"Let every soul be in subjection to the superior authorities, for there is no authority except by God; the existing authorities stand placed in their relative positions by God. Therefore he who opposes the authority has taken a stand against the arrangement of God; those who stand against it will receive judgement to themselves... For that is why you are also paying taxes; for they are God's public servants constantly serving this very purpose. Render to all their dues, to him who [calls for] the tax, the tax; to him who [calls for] the tribute, the tribute; to him who [calls for] fear,

such fear; to him who [calls for] honor, such honor." (verses 1-2, 6-7)

Jehovah's Witnesses believe they are doing well by adopting Bible values and teaching its version of morality to their children, but while claiming to love their children, they fail to protect them from abuse, covering up crimes against children in order to protect the reputation of their Organization. What is depressing about the situation highlighted by the Conti case, is that Jehovah's Witnesses seem incapable of recognizing that the policy of secrecy and the oppressive scriptural mores they place on their members are part of the problem, and that far from protecting their 'flock,' they are laying it wide open to abuse by unscrupulous predators within their ranks.

Their Organization suffers from the implementation of poor moral advice, sourced from within the pages of the Bible. It creates an environment in which reputation takes precedence over the welfare of individual members, including minors, and where emotional and physical abuse can take place behind closed doors.

Law and the pedophile

Compare the treatment of child abusers and their victims within the Organization of Jehovah's Witnesses, as explained above, with what happens if a suspected child abuser is convicted in a secular court of law.

After conviction in a secular court of law, pedophiles are dealt with by qualified professionals who ensure that they undergo a rigorous program devised to help them acknowledge their own guilt, recognize the extent of harm they have caused to their victim and to the families involved, and learn how to control their behavior. Having served their sentence, measures are taken to ensure that offenders do not take up residence in the vicinity of their victim or victims, and that the local authorities are informed of their whereabouts at all times.[92]

With respect to victims, in the UK they are entitled to assistance from the Witness Care Unit, and pre-trial therapy in the form of counseling and psychotherapy. They are not forced to confront their abuser, as would be the case with a judicial committee of elders. Instead, accompanied by a qualified supporter, they are able to speak from a live-link room adjacent to the court room. The wealth of organizations offering support and therapy to child abuse victims attests to the fact that this is an essential part of care.

The Organization of Jehovah's Witnesses does not measure up to these standards in any way.

Child abuse: Shunning

As we have learned, baptism lays children wide open and vulnerable to the charge of "falling short" if they fail to live up to their dedication vows. Scant concession is made due to their age. They face the prospect of being disfellowshipped even though they are minors. For children raised as Jehovah's Witnesses, this is an absolutely terrifying prospect, like being thrown to the dogs. Once disfellowshipped, *they are subject to much the same treatment as a fully grown adult.*

When disfellowshipped juveniles reach an age at which they are considered old enough to fend for themselves, parents shut the door on their own humanity and cut their children off completely, often by means of a phone call or an e-mail, informing them that they will have no further contact with them, and do not want anything more to do with them. When people on the outside learn of this behavior from those who have been treated in this manner, their usual reaction is one of shocked disbelief.

In a secular court of law, juveniles are not held fully responsible for their actions because they are minors, not adults. This is a precious distinction, which protects children from legal abuse. In the Organization of Jehovah's Witnesses, children have no such protection or rights as juveniles.

Shunning: Historical precedent

Shunning is hailed as a scriptural procedure that has the approval of God, and it is by no means unique to Jehovah's Witnesses. An edict of Byzantine Emperor Justinian (527-65CE), which effectively put an end to imperial toleration of religious beliefs other than orthodox

Christianity, was based on the same principle of exclusivity.

"All those who have not yet been baptised must come forward, whether they reside in the capital or in the provinces, and go to the very holy churches with their wives, their children, and their households, to be instructed in the true faith of Christianity. And once thus instructed and having sincerely renounced their former error, let them be judged worthy of redemptive baptism. Should they disobey, let them know that they will be excluded from the state and will no longer have any rights of possession, neither goods nor property; stripped of everything, they will be reduced to penury, without prejudice to the appropriate punishments that will be imposed upon them." [93]

The death penalty was meted out to those who stubbornly persisted with non- Christian practices.

Today, the same intolerance persists. With regard to the ongoing practice of shunning, *The Watchtower* article of April 15, 1988 states:

"Why is such a firm stand appropriate even today? Well, reflect on the severe cutting off mandated in God's Law to Israel. In various serious matters, wilful violators were executed. (Leviticus 20:10; Numbers 15:30, 31) When that happened, others, even relatives, could no longer speak with the dead lawbreaker. (Leviticus 19:1-4; Deuteronomy 13:1-5; 17:1-7) Though loyal Israelites back

244

then were normal humans with emotions like ours, they knew that God is just and loving and that his Law protected their moral and spiritual cleanness. So they could accept that his arrangement to cut off wrongdoers was fundamentally a good and right thing. – Job 34:10-12" [94]

How can the practice of murdering wrongdoers constitute an example of a "fundamentally good and right thing?" It makes sense when we understand that Jehovah's Witnesses occupy the same moral space as the ancient Israelites.

Shunning: the right to freedom of belief

Those who leave the Organization of Jehovah's Witnesses for conscientious reasons – because they are no longer in harmony with its beliefs and teachings or because they have decided that Christianity is not for them – are reviled as wicked people, "turning their backs on Jehovah." Such people are condemned to be shunned. Does this really make sense?

Recall the situation between the Apostles Paul and Peter. Each had strong beliefs, but despite the fact that they took opposing views on Christian conversion and even exchanged heated words on more than one occasion in public, did Paul shun Peter, or have him disfellowshipped for apostasy?

To adopt the Bible's moral values with respect to those who express disagreement, doubts, or have a change of heart, is to abandon the fundamental right to freedom of belief upheld by the United Nations Universal Declaration of Human Rights. I believe it is worth quoting it once more.

"Everyone has the right to freedom of thought, conscience and religion; this right includes freedom to change his religion or belief, and freedom, either alone or in community with others and in public or private, to manifest his religion or belief in teaching, practice, worship and observance."
  Article 18

Shunning: rights and family values

When only one partner in a marriage becomes a convert, strain is put on the marriage. The newly converted person is encouraged to "witness" to their partner despite their protests, and time spent together as a couple is eroded as the new convert attends various weekly meetings and uses previously free time on weekends to preach and distribute *The Watchtower* magazines either locally, or further afield. If the convert decides to enter the 'pioneer service' (full-time preaching from door to door), time together as a couple is further eroded. Add to this 'shepherding calls' (local elders' visits), and periodic days spent at local, circuit and district conventions, and it is not hard to see how their partners could become resentful.

When one baptized Witness partner does not agree with the accepted doctrine at any time after examining the evidence, what is the effect on the marriage and on the children? If such a person tries to teach their children in the way they now believe to be right, they are considered "opposed," and disfellowshipped. In other words, they are forced to choose between their beliefs and their family. Either they toe the line and deny their conscience, or stick to their principles and lose their family.

In the case of those who have been reproved or disfellowshipped but have family members who are still in "good standing" in the Organization, elders feel they have a right to enter their homes on "shepherding calls." They do not feel any obligation to request permission, even if the reproved person is considered to be the nominal head of the household. Any protest voiced by a "reproved" person is taken as "opposition," and grounds to disfellowship them. If they are already disfellowshipped, they are simply ignored. As a result, marriages come under enormous strain. In these cases, the Governing Body of Jehovah's Witnesses does not accept responsibility, nor does it express any remorse when break-ups occur and marriages are destroyed.

How can Jehovah's Witnesses believe that they uphold family life but then delegate all authority to the Organization to decide whether they may love their family or not? The society's practice of putting their religion before family, and their policy of shunning, disassociating, and disfellowshipping is responsible for acts of gross immorality against their own family members, including vulnerable children.

Shunning is unethical and immoral. It breeds intolerance on a par with fundamentalist Muslim countries where such dissenters incur the murderous hatred of the Muslim religious community.

Shunning: broken friendships

Prospective new members are led to believe they will find true friends and companions among Jehovah's Witnesses, an impression perpetuated under the heading in one of their recruitment brochures, *'How Does Associating with Fellow Christians Benefit Us?'*

"It builds lasting friendships. At our meeting, we gather together, not with mere acquaintances, but with a group of close friends. On other occasions, we spend time together in wholesome recreation. What beneficial effect does such association have? We learn to appreciate one another more, and that strengthens our bonds of love. Then, when our companions are facing problems, we readily help them because strong friendships have been established. (Proverbs 17:17) By associating with all members of our congregation, we show that we have 'the same care for one another.'- 1 Corinthians 12:25,26. We encourage you to choose as your friends those who are doing God's will. You will find such friends among

Jehovah's Witnesses. Please do not let anything hold you back from associating with us." [95]

Those who read the above carefully worded plea and join the Organization are impressed with its warmth, unaware that friendship is conditional. When they or their companions are "facing problems" with regard to their faith, their status is likely to change from "friend" to "enemy," literally overnight.

Shunning: the right to impartial judgement

Before anyone is disfellowshipped and shunned, they must attend a judicial hearing where they will meet with members of the judicial committee and face the accusations made against them. Jehovah's Witnesses believe that this internal justice system is effective because God's spirit operates upon the body of elders involved, thus guiding their decisions. In reality, it is an all-male committee of unqualified individuals who sit in judgement upon members of their own congregation. Such a committee is prone to be partial, and one or more of the elders on a committee is likely to be involved personally in the case under consideration. This makes the judicial process vulnerable to manipulation. Elders may use the judicial system to advance their own position, or garner support for making a case against those they consider a threat.

Judicial hearings take place in secret.   There is no representation for the accused.   There is no system of

249

appeal, no jury brought in from outside, and no members of the public or press invited in to witness its procedures. Minutes of judicial hearings are archived and not readily available for consultation. In short, such religiously-inspired internal judicial committees are the relic of a primitive, less effective system for administering justice.

The rights of women: Female subjection

The position of women within the Organization is one of submissiveness; they are held in check and prevented from assuming any responsible role apart from home building, child rearing, and swelling the ranks of publishers participating in the door-to-door ministry. Directing them to "keep silent" has resulted in a passive female membership that has no prospect of taking a share in the responsibilities of the day-to-day running of the Organization. They are excluded from such congregational duties as managing the congregational accounts, stocktaking, or even from mundane tasks like handling the roving microphones during the 'Watchtower Study.' Such discrimination does not bear the hallmark of wisdom, but merely reflects the outdated attitudes of centuries past.

Subjugated women are unaware that in the New Order, which they imagine will operate worldwide, their situation would deteriorate as fundamental human rights afforded them by the present system of secular government would be eroded or replaced with new, more

250

stringent restrictions enforced by the totalitarian Governing Body of Jehovah's Witnesses and its agencies.

The right to freedom of thought

"...The badness of man was abundant in the earth and every inclination of the thoughts of his heart was only bad all the time." Genesis 6:5

Can it be true freedom if God reads your thoughts and condemns you for them, even your inclinations? Just remember that because God read the thoughts of humans and decided they were "bad," he flooded the earth and drowned them all. Demonstrably, you must think only in a God-approved way, or else risk destruction at the hands of the Almighty. No doubt this is why parents are admonished to raise their children in the "*mental-regulating of Jehovah,*" (Ephesians 6:4) and why Paul speaks of "*bringing every thought into captivity.*" (2 Corinthians 10:5)

Anthony Morris III, a member of the Governing Body, describes independent thinking as "dangerous," an "'every man for himself' philosophy," and "something to be avoided." After describing Jehovah's Witnesses as "the thinkingest (sic) people on the planet," he warns them,

"What you have to be careful of, is don't let it become independent thinking."[96]

251

Attesting to the palpable lack of independent thinking, the commentary in a BBC documentary on Jehovah's Witnesses observes,

"...loyalty to the Watchtower Society has become a test of a person's fitness to survive Armageddon, so all Witnesses think and behave in the same manner." [97]

Tribal identity

Edward Wilson, professor emeritus at Harvard University, offers an additional explanation as to why total abnegation of independent thought and behavior is such a distinctive feature in human organizational arrangements like that of Jehovah's Witnesses.

"The early humans needed a story of everything important that happened to them because the conscious mind cannot work without stories and explanations of its own meaning. The best, the only way our forebears could manage to explain existence itself was a creation myth. And every creation myth, without exception, affirmed the superiority of the tribe that invented it over all other tribes. That much assumed, every religious believer saw himself as a chosen person. Organized religions and their gods, although conceived in ignorance of most of the real world, were unfortunately set in stone in early history. As in the beginning, they are everywhere still an expression of tribalism by which the members establish their own identity and special relation to the supernatural world. Their dogmas codify rules of behaviour that the devout can accept absolutely without hesitation. To question the sacred myths is to question the identity and worth of those who believe them. That is why sceptics, including those committed to different, equally absurd myths, are so righteously disliked. In some countries, they risk imprisonment or death." [98]

Admittedly, we are all products of our genetic inheritance, our country, and location at birth, and also our cultural, social, and ethnic background. Only a limited amount of free will is left to us as individuals. The Governing Body of Jehovah's Witnesses limits this freedom even further. Their version of "truth" ensures that its members are given no individual voice. There is no independence and no room for original thought.

The right to life: Medical science

Jehovah's Witnesses generally respect the medical profession and are agreeable to consultation with doctors and surgeons on matters of healthcare. Yet when the issue of blood or vaccines is raised, they begin to dictate terms, appearing to believe they have advanced medical and scientific knowledge that overrules recommendations for treatment from professional medical practitioners.

The arguments that Jehovah's Witnesses put forward to support their demands for alternative treatment are those approved by the Governing Body and disseminated via the pages of *The Watchtower* magazine or various booklets – also published by them – dealing with matters of medical concern. Those who fail to comply with the Governing Body's directives concerning medical treatment are considered to have disassociated themselves from the Organization of Jehovah's Witnesses, and are treated accordingly. As a result, they may find themselves shunned by their friends and family for disloyalty.

Whatever the Governing Body of Jehovah's Witnesses endorses as acceptable treatment is followed to the letter. Any treatment the Governing Body does not endorse is rejected regardless of the consequences, either to parents or to their children. The tragedy is that the Governing Body changes its mind concerning treatment for life-threatening conditions, so that Witnesses who have obediently refused a particular operation or course of treatment for their child in compliance with Governing Body directives may find that its guidelines have changed thereafter, and those treatments are now allowed.

Thousands of lives have been lost needlessly in this way, and yet the Governing Body makes no apology because it is convinced of its guidance by God's spirit. Surely the death of these loyal Witnesses lies squarely at the door of the Governing Body members involved, and should weigh heavily upon their consciences. It is perhaps surprising that more legal action has not been taken against the Governing Body on this issue.

The right of access to sources of information

The same ambivalent attitude exists towards professional historians, biologists, archeologists, paleontologists, geologists, vulcanologists, and other professionals who investigate the world around us and share what it can tell us about the past. The Jehovah's Witnesses' publications quote professionals in these fields of research in order to support their own arguments, but they are equally likely to ignore professional authorities when their findings fail to support what the Bible says, or what the Governing Body has decided is the case, or worse, they may take comments out of context to lend support to their argument.

A typical example can be found in the Watchtower Bible and Tract Society publication, '*Life – How did it get here? By evolution or by creation?*' in which a quote by Richard Dawkins appears on page 39.

"At this point a reader may begin to understand Dawkins' comment in the preface to his book [*The Selfish Gene*]: 'This book should be read almost as though it were science fiction.' But readers on the subject will find that his approach is not unique. Most other books on evolution also skim over the staggering problem of explaining the emergence of life from nonliving matter."

The reader is misled. What Dawkins actually wrote was,

"This book should be read almost as though it were science fiction. It is designed to appeal to the imagination. But it is not science fiction: it is science. *Cliché* or not, 'stranger than fiction' expresses exactly how I feel about the truth." [99]

Many more examples can be found in the same Watchtower Society publication to the extent that it calls into question their research methodology and lays them open to charges of deliberate manipulation of source material.

Instead of turning to primary sources of information, Witnesses are forced to rely on very limited and incomplete internal resources provided by those whom the Governing Body chooses to employ – namely, fellow Jehovah's Witnesses. Belief that these secondary sources of information are divinely approved blinds members to the reality of what has really been discovered about the world around us.

"The same yesterday, today, and forever" [100]

Many Jehovah's Witnesses believe that their Organization has always been consistent in its beliefs, teachings and behavior. They are unaware that the Governing Body keeps tight control of its own history. Those searching for information concerning the history of the Watchtower Bible and Tract Society or its defunct teachings will find that older copies of *The Watchtower* and *Awake!* magazines have disappeared from the Internet, and books printed by the Watchtower Bible and Tract Society have become unavailable.

The Governing Body revises its own history with various historical facts swept under the carpet (see the following sub-heading) and former teachings omitted (see 'Last Days'). Consequently, with public access to a dwindling supply of original sources of information, it is becoming more difficult to establish what revisions have been made. Obfuscation and manipulation of historical events is both cynical and immoral in an organization that claims to be scrupulously honest.

Political neutrality and a letter to Hitler

Jehovah's Witnesses claim political neutrality. They are adamant that they did not join in Christendom's support of the Second World War, and that they were the only body of Christians who, in all countries involved in that war, refused military service. For many Witnesses, the fact that it stood firm and united in its refusal to compromise its beliefs in the face of adversity, marks it as the only religion having God's approval. When confronted with doubts, perhaps concerning child abuse, the authenticity of the Bible, biblical morality or otherwise, many will dismiss them because they are convinced of the authenticity of the claim that Jehovah's Witnesses "stood up to Hitler" as a united body.

But is this claim true, or is it a founding myth?

Consider the following declaration, adopted by Jehovah's Witnesses during World War II.

Declaration of Facts, Trost, October 1943[101]

Every war brings countless misfortunes upon Mankind. Every war brings difficult moral dilemmas to thousands, yes, millions of people. This applies especially to this war, which has spared no corner of the earth and has been spread through the air, water and land. It is therefore inevitable that in such times, not only individuals, but also communities of every sort, unintentionally or deliberately are falsely suspected.

Even Jehovah's Witnesses have not been spared this fate. We have become made out to be an association, the object or activity of which is described as, "to undermine military discipline, especially to force or mislead conscripts into insubordination against military orders, neglect or refusal of duty, or becoming fugitives."

Such an opinion can only be put forward by someone who completely misunderstands the spirit and activity of our Society or who despite his better knowledge, malevolently distorts it.

We expressly state, that our association neither commands nor recommends, nor in any other way suggests, acting against military orders. Questions of that sort are dealt with neither by our congregations nor in the Society's published literature. We do not at all concern ourselves with such questions. We view our business to

258

be solely that of rendering a witness to Jehovah God and to proclaim bible truth to all peoples. Hundreds of our members and fellow believers have performed their military duty and continue to do so.

We have at no time presumed and at no time shall do so, to view the performance of military duty, as laid down by your statutes, as an offence against the principles and aspirations of the association of Jehovah's Witnesses. We beseech all our members and fellow believers, in the proclamation of the message of God's Kingdom (Matthew 24:14), to confine themselves strictly to the proclamation of bible truth, and always to avoid giving grounds for misunderstanding, and certainly never to be able to be misunderstood as offering any incitement to insubordination against military orders. [*Italics mine*]

Swiss Association of Jehovah's Witnesses
President: Ad. Gammenthaler; Secretary: D.
Wiedenmann. Berne, 15th September 1943

An estimated two hundred and fifty German Jehovah's Witnesses were executed – mostly after being tried and convicted by military tribunals – for refusing to serve in the German military, precisely because they believed the performance of military duties was indeed "an offense against the principles and aspirations of the association of Jehovah's Witnesses." Thousands more Witnesses died in Nazi concentration camps for the same reason over the course of the war. What would they have thought, had they known that their Swiss counterparts had been encouraged to take a different stance entirely?

Jehovah's Witnesses also claim to be the only religious body to "stand up to Hitler" by refusing to support the war effort or take up arms against their fellows in other countries involved in the war. They claim to have remained completely neutral throughout the build-up to the conflict, and during the war itself. However, on the 25th June 1933, more than 7,000 of Jehovah's Witnesses assembled at Berlin and unanimously adopted a resolution. Millions of copies of the accepted resolution – now boldly renamed a 'declaration' – were subsequently printed and distributed throughout Germany. A copy of the declaration together with a covering letter was delivered to Hitler. The declaration includes the following (translated) statement, under the heading, 'Juden' (Jews):

"It is falsely charged by our enemies that we have received financial support for our work from the Jews. Nothing is farther from the truth. Up to this hour there never has been the slightest bit of money contributed to our work by Jews. We are the faithful followers of Christ Jesus and believe upon Him as the Savior of the world, whereas the Jews entirely reject Jesus Christ and emphatically deny that he is the Savior of the world sent of God for man's good. This of itself should be sufficient proof to show that we receive no support from Jews and that therefore the charges against us are maliciously false and could proceed only from Satan, our great enemy.

"The greatest and the most oppressive empire on earth is the Anglo-American empire. By that is meant the British Empire, of which the United States of America forms a part. It has been the commercial Jews of the British-American empire that have built up and carried on Big Business as a means of exploiting and oppressing the peoples of many nations. This fact particularly applies to the cities of London and New York, the stronghold of Big Business. This fact is so manifest in America that there is a proverb concerning the city of New York which says: 'The Jews own it, the Irish Catholics rule it, and the Americans pay the bills.' We have no fight with any of these persons mentioned, but, as the witnesses for Jehovah and in obedience to his commandment set forth in the Scriptures, we are compelled to call attention to the truth concerning the same in order that the people may be enlightened concerning God and his purpose."[102] [103]

Is this neutrality? Jehovah's Witnesses seem to have forgotten that they worship the same God as the Jews, Jehovah. How then, can they justify joining in the prevailing *zeitgeist* against the Jews? Surely, this is the most objectionable hypocrisy, a clear case of washing their hands like Pontius Pilate, in order to ingratiate themselves with the German Führer. (Matthew 27:15-24)

Hedonism

Jehovah's Witnesses believe that they are peaceable people with a healthy respect for life, but as we have seen from our discussion of Armageddon, while claiming to love other people and expending time in 'field service' in order to save them, they fully expect the violent death of 99.9% of humanity, praying earnestly for it to come in their lifetime.

Their Governing Body takes the lead in encouraging them to believe that they are "*a people for special possession,*" the sole organization approved by God.   Exclusivity is responsible for fomenting a self-righteous and intolerant attitude towards those on the outside. It is a manifestation of tribalism – the "us" and "them" mentality we discussed earlier – that is both alienating and inappropriate in any civilized setting.

Since Jehovah's Witnesses believe that it is impossible to be a good person without the fear of divine punishment, the question arises as to whether they are good simply because they are afraid of the consequences of disobedience. At the same time, in return for their good behaviour, hedonists within their ranks are obsessed with winning the prize of eternal life and in living on earth forever, replete with the kind of luxurious homes and conditions that ordinary people could never afford.

"You'll see how God these things supplies, If you keep your eyes on the prize." [104]

In contrast, many whom they describe as "worldly" people are good simply because they want to be good, with no thought of reward. This is borne out by scientific studies that have shown that altruism is inbuilt in humans and also manifests itself in a number of other species.[105]

Time Magazine, commenting on the Pew Forum on Religion and Public Life, reports that two-thirds of 'born-ins' – children born into the Organization of Jehovah's Witnesses – eventually leave, despite the trauma this entails.[106] Having been taught all their lives to hate and fear the world outside the doors of the Kingdom Hall, they discover the truth contained in an observation made in George Orwell's novel, *1984.*

> "If [an ordinary citizen] were allowed contact with foreigners he would discover that they are creatures similar to himself and that most of what he has been told about them is lies. The sealed world in which he lives would be broken, and the fear, hatred, and self-righteousness on which his morale depends might evaporate."

Plans for a New Order

While decrying the injustices of this world and yearning for a just new world, the Governing Body of Jehovah's Witnesses intends to model the New Order on their existing system of justice. The Governing Body will therefore:

- merge the judiciary system with a New World government so that government members can control the outcome of any court cases,

- abolish trial by jury, and
- strip away the defendant's right to legal representation.

In contrast, Article 10 of the Universal Declaration of Human Rights states:

> "Everyone is entitled in full equality to a fair and public hearing by an independent and impartial tribunal, in the determination of his rights and obligations and of any criminal charge against him."

Article 11(1) continues,

> "Everyone charged with a penal offence has the right to be presumed innocent until proved guilty according to law in a public trial at which he has had all the guarantees necessary for his defence."

Which seems to you to be the higher moral option?

In the New World Order, the Governing Body of Jehovah's Witnesses will abolish democracy so that the Governing Body and appointed congregational elders will have absolute power and will not be accountable to anyone. They will re-introduce the death penalty for a very long list of crimes, including reading the wrong type of book, harboring independent thoughts, or changing beliefs.

Truth

> *"...and you will know the truth, and the truth will set you free."* John 8:33

Jehovah's Witnesses believe that the original 'sin' of Adam and Eve was to decide good and bad for themselves, rather than being obedient to God. It is seen as an issue of free will. God explained the principle when addressing the Israelites.

> *"... I have put life and death before you, the blessing and the malediction; and you must choose life in order that you may keep alive, you and your offspring."* *Deuteronomy 30:19*

> *"In case you should leave Jehovah and you do serve foreign gods, he also will certainly turn back and do you injury and exterminate you after he has done you good."* *Joshua 24:20*

Those "choosing" to serve Jehovah give up any claim of "knowing good and bad" for themselves. (Genesis 3:22, 23) Instead, they allow themselves to be dictated to in every avenue of their lives by those claiming to speak on God's behalf.

Making decisions and choices is about responsibility, and taking responsibility for our own actions is a far cry from choosing a particular path in order to avoid punishment for non-compliance, or abnegating responsibility in order to conform to outdated edicts and injunctions from a small body of men who claim divine authority.

The Governing Body of Jehovah's Witnesses operates under a system of fossilized Roman politics founded on the edicts of Constantine (a man who murdered members of his own family), and on fourth and fifth-century bishops who used Christianity as a political tool to gain power and authority for themselves. The benefits of modern democracy are swept aside in favor of morally inferior policies, procedures, principles, and standards.

Policymakers and Jehovah's Witnesses

Freedom of religion is upheld in the Universal Declaration of Human Rights, but there are questions that can be asked as to how far that freedom can be allowed to impinge on the rights of others.

In fact, over the centuries, Western societies have regulated the more damaging religious practices. Human sacrifice, once widely practiced in some cultures, is classed as ritual murder and has long been abolished. In India, *sati*, or *suttee* – the self-immolation of a Hindu widow on her husband's funeral pyre – was banned by the British in 1829. Honor killings are not permitted in our society, neither is burning at the stake, or stoning to death.

Following the 9/11 and 7/7 terrorist attacks, some politicians have been questioning whether freedom of religion has gone too far, and whether further regulation is needed to protect others in society. In the UK, new legislation outlawing the incitement of religious hatred was introduced in 2006. A recent test of this legislation involved the radical Islamist cleric, Abu Hamza, extradited from Britain in October 2012 to the United States to face charges of soliciting murder and inciting racial hatred.

Delivering his original sentence in the UK, the judge, Mr Justice Hughes, said Hamza had,

"...helped to create an atmosphere in which to kill has become regarded by some as not only a legitimate course but a moral and religious duty in pursuit of perceived justice." [107]

Whilst Jehovah's Witnesses do not expect to commit acts of murder or genocide personally at the present time, we have seen that there are some features of their Organization that do have, or potentially could have, an adverse effect on society at large.

To summarize:-

- *The Watchtower* publications contain defamatory material concerning other religions and so-called apostates that could be understood as incitement of religious hatred. Is the practice of demonizing society and praying for the death of 99.9% of earth's citizens appropriate in a civilized society?
- Jehovah's Witnesses operate a 'state within a state,' having their own laws, law courts, and punishments that do not measure up to the standards of civilized society. This has caused many problems, including

267

the protection of sexual abusers and the prohibition of specific life-saving medical treatments to those in need.

- The policy of denying children access to wider association, combined with the enforced shunning of minors, is a form of emotional abuse.
- Shunning is divisive, breaking families apart.

The eight members of the Governing Body of Jehovah's Witnesses exercise a level of totalitarian control over their nearly eight-million-strong flock that is almost unprecedented in human history. We have already seen how they can deny access to vital medical treatment for their members and change their criteria, almost at a whim. The number of deaths that have resulted directly from these changes – and those that are yet to occur – may never be known.

We can be grateful that the Governing Body does not currently advocate its members to use violence, preferring to leave retribution to God, but policymakers may wish to consider whether this situation is stable. Whereas previous generations of the Governing Body comprised individuals who were raised in the real world and had the benefit of at least some secular education, the future Governing Body is more likely to be comprised entirely of individuals who are raised from birth within the Organization of Jehovah's Witnesses. Their earliest educational memories will be of internal publications containing illustrations depicting the mass execution of the human race.

Consider the many instances in history of religious leaders leading their flocks to disaster – examples include Jim Jones who orchestrated the mass suicide and murder of over 900 members of the People's Temple in 1978, and Joseph di Mambro who, together with Luc Jouret, were responsible for murder and mass suicide within the Order of the Solar Temple in 1994.

Should a charismatic and ruthless individual gain control of the Governing Body of Jehovah's Witnesses, he would find himself with almost unlimited power over a worldwide following of millions of highly motivated, obedient people.

Whilst cherishing the right of Jehovah's Witnesses, alongside all other people of faith, to practice their religion in freedom, policymakers might want to consider the way in which Jehovah's Witnesses use shunning as the principle means to exercise absolute control over their members. It is possible that, by removing this one powerful tool, the Governing Body would cease to be a potential threat to society.

Regulation to prevent shunning, while weakening the level of control the Governing Body exercises over its flock, would:

- reduce the number of cases where Witnesses refuse vital medical treatment for fear of being shunned,

- improve the lives of millions of children who suffer emotional trauma following shunning by parents, and

- reduce the number of families split apart by Society policies.

Serious thought should also be given to legislation and the application of laws dealing with incitement to religious hatred, to curtail the more aggressive language used in organizational literature and public speaking aimed at former members and other religious groups.

REALITY

The Pacific Islands

Blue. Nothing but pale, glaring blue above my head, filling the sky in every direction, its smooth walls touching the rim of the sea rippling beneath my raft. Only the Heads are visible; massive wedges of granite hunched together. The island that anchors them has disappeared from sight, and they look as if they stand once more upon the bed of the ocean, free to wander where they will.

The Ancient Ones believe that in ages past the Heads fell from the sky down to the darkest reaches of the deep. Power surged within them and they stood and lifted their heads above the waters and walked about until they grew old and tired of wandering. When they were still at last, the island grew up around them while they dreamed. Time drifted over them until their souls returned to the sky.

Only when we, the Chieftains of our tribe return every year to consult with them, do the invisible gods inhabit the Heads once more and talk to the sons of men. We arrive in a sturdy boat laden with gifts, drawing it up high on the leeward side of the island, sheltered from the buffeting wind. Silently, we take our places within the company of waiting Heads, preparing ourselves for the revelations that will come. We drape our garlands of ripe fruits and flowers around each Head in turn, then pour out wine upon the sacred ground and offer up our prayers. We listen to our breathing, watch, and await the spirits of the gods with fear.

Blue. Colored pigment rubbed into our faces and bodies until we resemble the granite of the Heads. We pass the ceremonial Shell between us and drink deeply of its bitter liquid as the dying sun buries itself in the heart of a golden sea. The bruised clouds darken and swell, casting their monstrous shadows over the water. The wind rushes in on us and the faces of the Heads shift and turn, their eyes black with the ancient knowledge meant only for us, the initiated ones. When they speak, the heavens crack open and the ground trembles. Thunder roars, the waters of ocean and sky collide and we are drowning on the land, standing in the sea, walking with the gods.

Sleep. I must sleep. My raft sways and dips. I am curled up like an unborn child deep inside the womb. The sun warms my back like a comforting hand. I am cast adrift...

"Rangi," my mother's voice whispers in the tunnels of my mind. "Rangi, you ask too many questions. Do you not know that not every question has an answer?"

My childhood self frowns and kicks the dirt, unable to believe there can possibly be unanswerable questions. My mother smiles and places her basket of fruits on the ground beside her.

"The Chieftains are there to guide us, Rangi. They speak with the Heads and bring their words back to us. It is enough for us to follow them." She stoops and ruffles

272

my hair. "One day you will be a Chieftain too, you'll see. Then you will consult with the Heads yourself, and you will know everything." She picks up her basket, holds out her hand to me, and together we walk back home.

Regret. My adult self, rocking in the swell, recalls my mother's gentle ignorance with sadness and regret. I think, momentarily, that if I had not become a Chieftain I might have been content to be a sea trader like my brother. Deep down, I know that is a lie. I was not content. Not as a boy, and not as a young man. Nothing could stop me from working my way into the good graces of the Chieftains. I wanted all my questions answered, and the only way to do that was to become one with those who consulted the Heads.

At first, when I saw the Heads awaken and heard their voices speak of sacred knowledge, all my doubts were swept aside. Then, after a while, the whisperings of uncertainty came creeping back into the corners of my mind and would not leave, no matter how hard I tried to shut them out. I vowed to myself that when the next ceremony on the island of the Heads took place, I would discover the truth.

So it came about. Once the ceremonial ritual was initiated and the Shell was passed around, I simulated drinking my fill, but in truth, I swallowed nothing. Surely if the gods truly inhabited the Heads, they would communicate with me directly, without assistance. We raised our hands and we prayed. We implored the spirits of the gods to inhabit the Heads and speak with us once

273

more. The carved faces remained immobile. Again we passed around the Shell, and again, I drank nothing. Now I could see a change, not in the faces of the Heads, but in those of the other Chieftains. Their eyes started out of their sockets and their contorted mouths formed words that made no sense. Still the earth did not shake, and the sky remained as calm and clear as it had been when we had run our boat ashore. The Heads did not speak. The Chieftains heard nothing but the voices of their own minds. The silence was more dreadful than any imagining. I implored the spirits to enter into me and fill me with their sacred knowledge, but instead, confusion and distress gripped me, and still the Heads did not speak.

Truth. The truth is that there is no wisdom in the Heads. My sullen silence did not go unnoticed by my fellow Chieftains and before too long the truth was coaxed out of me. They were enraged that I had disgraced myself before the Heads and hauled me before the Judgement Seat. I was condemned as a traitor who contaminated the purity of the sacred and turned his back on the gods. The outcome was inevitable. Banished from the tribe, suddenly everyone despised me; even my brother and my friends deserted me, and all I had once held dear was ripped away from me.

The Chieftains dragged me through the village and down to the water's edge. No one dared emerge from their huts to watch as our small procession wound its way between them, our feet moving in time to the beat of a drum, slow and insistent. Even my mother, once so proud of me, was nowhere to be seen. I could feel my heart beat faster as we passed close by the hut in which I lived with my wife and children. I longed to see them one last time before leaving the village forever. I hoped that perhaps they would come running out to see me even now, but there was no sound from within.

A sturdy boat hung upon the tide close to shore, waiting to take us out to the Heads. As we waded through the shallows, I scanned the shoreline for any sign of my family, but in my heart I knew the beach would be deserted. Rough hands manhandled me onto a raft that was strapped to the boat with strips of leather. In silence the Chieftains rowed out to the island where the Heads could witness my Judgement and see me cast adrift on the ocean current.

The sun darkens, the wind rises and the Heads disappear behind the rising swell. Adrift... I am cast adrift...

I awake to find that the tide has swept me past the island on the eastern side, but now I sense, rather see, on the edge of my vision a thickening of the horizon that might be something, or nothing.

The voice of the Storyteller, my mother, whispers to her child.

"Beyond the Heads lies another island much larger than ours, but barren, inhabited by demons, mortal enemies of the Heads. Envious of the Heads' power and wisdom, the demons sought to destroy them. Battles raged for untold ages until the sea boiled and the sky burned red

275

with fury, but in the end, the demons were defeated and banished to an island away from the face of the gods. We know it as A'inakua - The Forbidden Land, the Land of Demons."

The voice fades to no more than the sound of water lapping against the side of the raft, but my imagination fills the space beyond the horizon. If the Heads have no power, then neither do the demons of A'inakua. Is it possible that they do not even exist? If that is so, then there is nothing to fear.

Strange to think that I have been afraid all my life and never realized it until now. But if, as I suspect, the tide is carrying me towards that distant land beyond the horizon, I might at last leave my doubts and fears behind me and dare to step ashore.

***

The bigger picture

It was once thought that our tiny planet was at the center of everything. The Sun and all the lesser heavenly bodies moved in a graceful arc around it. Beyond the canopy of the star-studded heavenly dome lay the invisible realm of God.

We have come a long way from that geocentric view. We understand now that our small planet is not at the center of the universe. It does not even occupy the center of our solar system. That honor goes to the Sun, but it does not end there. We have been humbled to discover that our solar system is not at the center of the universe either. Our average-sized sun is hovering on an outer arm of the Milky Way galaxy, only one of roughly two hundred billion balls of burning gas scattered across it. Nor is the Milky Way at the center of the universe. Powerful optics has identified hundreds of millions of galaxies in great clusters and swoops all around us, some of them far larger than our galaxy. Our universe is unimaginably vast.

Viewed from this perspective, our planet contains the only intelligent life forms we know of at the present time in our universe. Humans are all members of the same family, living on the same infinitesimally small planet whirling in the immensity of space. Does it make any sense for a small fraction of this tiny planet's population to imagine itself selected for special favor at the expense of the majority of its fellow members? Surely it makes better sense to recognize that love, empathy, and compassion should not be reserved for a tiny portion of earth's human family. We will not make the world a better place by setting ourselves apart from our fellows because they do not share exactly the same beliefs as we do. Nor will we improve the world by violent genocide at the hands of a jealous deity. Instead, we can each do our part to improve things by our actions now, by changing our attitude, widening out, by being willing to see and appreciate the good in all people, and by each doing what we can to leave the world a better place than we found it.

It is hubris to think that our current understanding of the world is the whole truth, the ultimate reality, the true nature of what is really out there. In terms of understanding our world, we humans are near the start of a very long journey. We must be open to new discoveries that challenge our way of thinking and avoid the temptation to lapse into dogmatism given how little we currently know. A.C. Grayling observes,

"All the enquiries that human intelligence conducts with the aim of enlarging knowledge always make progress at the cost of generating new questions. Having the intellectual courage to live with open-endedness and uncertainty, trusting to reason and experiment to gain us increments of understanding, having the integrity to base one's views on rigorous and testable foundations, and being committed to changing one's mind when shown to be wrong, are the marks of honest minds." [108]

Humans' place in the environment

Turning to the different life forms on planet earth, it is not healthy to imagine that everything revolves around us humans, as if we were the pinnacle of creation. In truth, the five senses that we humans use to interact with the world around us are quite limited in scope. Animal behaviorists are only now discovering the richness of language used by other species. Many animals and birds communicate with sounds that are outside the range of the human ear. Bats 'see' in total darkness because they use echolocation, undetectable to us. They emit sounds that bounce off objects, enabling them to navigate accurately in restricted locations, in total darkness, despite the proximity of thousands of other mobile bats swirling around them. They can detect and locate their own offspring out of millions occupying the caves they inhabit. Whales, dolphins, and other marine creatures also use echolocation to locate predators and prey. Eagles have powerful telescopic vision. Nocturnal animals' ability to see in the dark is far superior to ours. Our sense of smell is rudimentary compared to that of hunting animals that track their prey by following their scent.

Even livestock, which many people consider non-sentient, bred solely for the purpose of feeding humans, have demonstrated remarkable cognitive ability. For example, according to a study on cognition in sheep conducted by K.M. Kendrick of the Department of Cognitive and Behavioural Neuroscience at the Babraham Institute, Cambridge, not only can sheep recognize at least fifty faces of their own kind and ten human faces at any one time, but they also show signs of remembering specific sheep and humans after absences of several years.[109]

When we uncover some of the amazing abilities of even the most lowly of our fellow creatures, we are challenged to reshape our thinking and attitudes. We come to appreciate that their perspective of the world is just as valid as ours, and that they have as much right to life on this planet as we do. They do not exist for our benefit, and we have no right to exploit them or destroy their habitats. This should give us a strengthened sense of balance, of recognizing our place in the scheme of things, not at the apex of a pyramid in which we imagine all other species placed below us, but as an integral part of a diverse planet.

It takes humility to accept the fact that human beings possess no special status in the Holocene. Instead, freedom from preconceived ideas about rights and privileges opens up recognition of the genuine accountability and personal responsibility we need to extend towards all who share our living environment. Selfishness gives way to generosity of spirit and the realisation that there is no valid basis for denying any of our fellow humans, or other species, the benefit of our empathy and compassion.

The tyranny of immortality

Nothing is more certain to cause dissatisfaction with life than a belief that immortality has been snatched away from us. The conviction that our 'real' lives lie yet ahead, after this life has been cast aside, that the current world and all life on it is somehow degenerate, or that our disabilities and imperfections will be miraculously 'fixed' by the Almighty in a future paradise, inevitably detracts from the life we are living here and now. It prevents us from appreciating the qualities of others and of the wonderful world we live in; it discourages us from working to better the lives of our fellow humans (and animals), and it prevents us from making the most of our own lives.

Consider our attitude towards our own old age. To those who yearn for immortality in the New Order, the 'declining years' are viewed as a regrettable deterioration in the human condition, the sad and inevitable consequence of sin and imperfection. However, recent trends are questioning popular assumptions about older people, their outlook on life, and their place in society.

Psychologist, Laura Carstensen, Director of the Stanford Center on Longevity, has conducted extensive studies on how extended lifetimes affect well-being. In a 2011 TED lecture,[110] she explains that an increase in life expectancy is a remarkable product of culture, and that the perception that it is a "sweeping downward course" is grossly inaccurate. Ageing brings some remarkable improvements in quality of life; for instance, increased knowledge and expertise. Emotional aspects of life also improve. Study after study confirms that older people are happier than middle-aged and younger people. Stress, worry, and anger all decrease with age.

Carstensen observes, "Recognizing that we won't live forever changes our perspective on life in positive ways." Time horizons grow shorter. As people age, they are better able to gauge their priorities and take less notice of trivialities. They invest in the more emotionally important aspects of life. They are also more appreciative and open to reconciliation. In short, they savor life. As a result, life gets better and they are happier day to day. At the same time, "the shift in their perspective leads them to have less tolerance than ever for injustice."

What are the implications for societies with a growing population of older people? Carstensen believes that if they are willing to capitalize on the strengths of the older generation,

"Societies with millions of talented, emotionally stable citizens who are healthier and better educated than any generations before them, armed with knowledge about the practical matters of life and motivated to solve the big issues, can be better societies than we have ever known."

While those still suffering from disability, or other physical or mental trauma, would wish for respite or restoration of their bodies to the perfection promised in the Bible, free from old age and death, the question to consider is whether the price demanded by God is worth it. Would personal preservation be worth the sacrifice of family life, and at the expense of 99.9 percent of earth's inhabitants?

We should be glad that many individuals from earlier generations were willing to put aside selfish desire for eternal life or tribal exclusiveness in order to devote their energies to making the world a better place. Civilization is a remarkable achievement, built up over thousands of years. We have every reason to celebrate and be thankful for all the good things we have inherited due to the unceasing efforts of those others who have struggled and fought to improve the lot of their fellow human beings. Aspects of human life on earth that we all admire – beautiful landscapes, architecture, sculpture, music, art, technological achievements, and medical and scientific advancements – are available for most of us to enjoy now, but we are only able to benefit from these achievements because of the freedom of people from diverse cultures and backgrounds that has allowed them to associate and collaborate together. They have done this in a spirit of mutual enquiry and cooperation, resulting in shared knowledge, which is inclusive, not exclusive.

The knowledge – including research and expertise – that has been amassed by those who have gone before us in every field of human endeavor is not withheld from us, closely guarded under exclusive rights of ownership. It is largely accessible to those who take the time and trouble to seek it out.

One might question the idea that the world is full of bad people. If you look for badness, you will surely find it, but if you let go of prejudices, you will find that the world is full of honest-hearted people. There is genuine kindness, compassion, empathy, and concern all around you, but if you are looking the other way, encouraged to focus on all that is negative in the world, you will not find them.

Allowing ourselves to associate freely with those from other walks of life ushers in a colorful world full of genuine friends; our lives are the richer because we have extended hospitality to those with different points of view, different backgrounds, and different experiences in life. Meeting people who do not all *speak in agreement... in the same mind and in the same line of thought"* (1 Corinthian 1:10) stretches our minds, stimulating our mental faculties, leading to new ideas and fresh ways of doing things.

Almost everyone appreciates the value of qualities such as empathy, compassion, altruism, tolerance, sympathy, forbearance, self-control, kindness, and patience. These are virtues, universally recognized as such, because in an imperfect world they take effort to cultivate, often in the face of adversity.

Paradise

Leaving aside the suspect morals and organizational structure of the proposed New World order, it is doubtful that eternal life in a paradise earth could ever live up to its promise of eternal happiness.

In a perfect world, how would empathy, compassion, altruism, tolerance, sympathy, forbearance, self-control, kindness, and patience be recognized and appreciated as virtues? If you consider the circumstances under which each of the above virtues might apply, you will realize that most of them would not even be necessary in a faultless world. Imagine if humans no longer had any necessity to cultivate such virtues. What kind of world would that be?

In a world populated with perfect people who will never grow old, the eventuality is that childbearing will no longer be necessary and sexual relations will become obsolete. Since the differences between the sexes are largely determined on the basis of procreation, the physiological, psychological, and emotional makeup of humans will be certain to change substantially. In a world without death, humans will become more androgynous as the distinctive physical features we associate with masculinity and femininity fade and eventually disappear. Those living in such a world will bear no children; they will never become parents or grandparents. The whole basis of family life will collapse. What then, will give life meaning?

The reality is that eternal life is unlikely to usher in unending happiness for Armageddon survivors. What is needed is simply a matter of gaining the right perspective on the life we have here and now. If we were to visit almost any era in earth's history up until a hundred years ago and describe to its inhabitants the quality of life in a democracy today – better health care, life expectancy, housing, food production, education, and reduced crime, violence, and discrimination, they would think it almost a paradise.

Millions now living would have died had they lived in a previous century. Using the field of medicine as an example, ignorance concerning hygiene accounted for the spread of infectious diseases. Conditions that today require only routine treatment or surgery were once either seriously debilitating or fatal. A detached retina, repaired with laser surgery as an outpatient, would have caused blindness in the not-so-distant past. Broken bones would often result in victims spending the rest of their days disabled and immobile. During the last one hundred years alone there have been extensive, life-changing advances in treatment. An ectopic pregnancy, a brain tumor, a hole in the heart, or even a heart attack no longer means certain death and, as we have seen, vaccines have eliminated many deadly viruses. A growing area of expertise is in prenatal surgery, pioneered in the 1980s.

286

With the aid of advanced technology, fetal imaging and prenatal testing, it is possible to detect and correct many defects *in utero*, including *sacrococcygeal teratoma* (a potentially fatal tumor that grows at the base of the spine) and *spina bifida/myelomeningocele*.

These medical treatments have been discovered through the scientific method, and there is every reason to be confident that more of the life-threatening illnesses and diseases that remain with us may be eradicated within our lifetime or that of the next generation, possibly most forms of cancer, heart disease, arthritis, Alzheimer's disease, and Parkinson's disease. There has been no need for miraculous intervention to address these problems, and no exclusive society membership is demanded of patients before they can benefit.

Thousands of able-bodied people living out their lives today would have been disabled had they lived only fifty years ago. Herein lies the real hope for Elsa, whom we met in our introduction. Elsa's best hope for the future is in the continuation of scientific progress, and it can be achieved without any need for divine interference.

No one would argue with the fact that there is still a long way to go, but some, like biologist and naturalist, Edward O. Wilson, are cautiously optimistic.

"Earth, by the twenty-second century, can be turned, if we so wish, into a permanent paradise for human beings, or at least the strong beginnings of one. We will do a lot of damage to ourselves and the rest of life along the way, but out of an ethic of simple decency to one another, the unrelenting application of reason, and the acceptance of what we truly are, our dreams will finally come home to stay." [111]

How will you live your life?

We have ample reason to be grateful for the gift of life on our beautiful planet Earth. True happiness and fulfillment can be found in appreciating and learning from those of different backgrounds and beliefs with an open mind. Joy can be had from learning about the fascinating and diverse species with which we share our planet. Self-knowledge can be enhanced by the ongoing discoveries that are peeling back the layers of history behind our own species.

Each of us is accountable to our fellow humans and other species on our planet. We can use our lives to do as much as we can to make all our lives better. The 'ship' is not sinking, and we should not leave everyone else to 'paint the funnel' while we sit by and complain. Nothing can be achieved by setting ourselves apart from the world. In order to help others we must fully engage with society and its institutions. As responsible individuals, we can use whatever skills and talents we have to help our fellow creatures, and to do our part, however small, in helping to make this world a better place for future generations.

We are already privileged in a sense far removed from the biblical meaning of the term. We find ourselves here, at this unique juncture in time, with a choice set squarely before us. Will we live out the rest of our lives in a state of fault-finding ingratitude? Will we ignore our full potential and our wider social context in the vain hope that perfection will be bestowed upon us? Or will we embrace reality, accept who we really are, and make the most of what we have, recognizing that now is the perfect moment?

---

[1] All Bible quotations are from the *New World Translation of the Holy Scriptures*, published by the Watchtower Bible and Tract Society of New York Inc., unless otherwise stated.

References

Morality

[2] *Orations Against the Jews.*

[3] Meeting with Bishop Wilhelm Berning of Osnabrück, representative of the German Bishops' Conference, 26 April, 1933.

[4] *The Real North Korea: Life and Politics in the Failed Stalinist Utopia*, Andrei Lankov, Oxford University Press USA, 2013. See pages 41-42

[5] Sam Harris, *Letter to a Christian Nation*, Pub. A.A. Knopf, New York, 2006, p.14

[6] Trials in which God was expected to intervene if the accused was innocent. For example, the cold water test in which the accused was bound hand and foot and plunged into a river. If he drowned, he was guilty, but if he floated unharmed, he was proved innocent.

[7] http://travel.state.gov/travel/cis_pa_tw/cis/cis_1056.html#criminal_penalties

[8] *Chicago Tribune, Business*, 'As Muslims rage, churches hit Pakistan blasphemy law,' Robert Evans, Reuters, 17 September, 2012.

[9] http://www.asafeworldforwomen.org/womens-rights/report-iran-execution-of-women-and-children/iran-execution-of-women-and-children/execution-of-children.html

[10] OLR Research Report, 'Death Penalty,' 31 July 2012.

Violence

[11] SW Africa Radio, The Annual World's 10 Worst Dictators, David Wallechinsky, Jan. 22, 2006. www.swradioafrica.com

[12] *Apply Yourself to Reading*, be p.21-p.26, par. 5, Watchtower Online Library

[13] Jared Diamond, *The World Until Yesterday. What Can We Learn From Traditional Societies? 2012*

[14] *Gerald of Wales*, Trans. Lewis Thorpe, Penguin Classics, 1978

[15] Ibid. page 80

[16] Ibid. page 78

[17] *Conquistadors*, Michael Wood, 2000 p.20

[18] Blainey, Geoffrey, *A Land Half Won*, Macmillan, South Melbourne, Vic., 1980, p.75

Bible Canon

[19] *Ante-Nicene Fathers, Volume IV, Part 4*, 'On the Apparel of Women,' Book 1. Circa AD 202

[20] Acts of Thecla, verse 37

[21] Acts of Thecla, verse 43

[22] Bart D. Ehrman, *Lost Christianities*, Oxford University Press, 2003, p.97

[23] See *The Cult of St Thecla, a tradition of women's piety in Late Antiquity,* Stephen J. Davis, Oxford Early Christian Studies series, Oxford University Press, 2008

[24] 'Saint Thecla,' *Encyclopaedia Romana, Rome, The Home of Empire and of All Perfection,* Essays on the History and Culture of Rome.
http://penelope.uchicago.edu/~grout/encyclopaedia_romana/glad iators/thecla.html

[25] Charles Freeman, *The Closing of the Western Mind. The Rise of Faith and the Fall of Reason,* Pimlico, 2003 p.154-5

[26] Metzger, Bruce M. *The Canon of the New Testament: Its Origin, Development and Significance*. Oxford: Clarendon, 1987, p.315

[27] Ross Shepard Kraemar, *Her Share of the Blessings: Women's Religions Among Pagans, Jews, And Christians in the Greco-Roman World.* Oxford University Press, 1992, p.7

[28] Bart D. Ehrman, *Forged*, HarperOne, 2011

[29] *Bible for Learners*, Vol. III, Philip Henry Wicksteed, et al. (2010) p.23

[30] Lost Christianities, p.234-235

[31] New Jerusalem Bible, p.2028

[32] *Ibid.*, p.242

Last Days

[33] World English Bible

[34] *When Prophecy Fails*, Leon Festinger, H.W. Riecken, S. Schachter, 2008 (Reprint of 1956 edition), p.4

[35] 'Come Be My Follower,' Watchtower Bible and Tract Society of Pennsylvania, 2007, p.185

[36] The *Watchtower* is the principal monthly magazine of Jehovah's Witnesses, published by the Watchtower Bible and Tract Society of Pennsylvania.

[37] Andrew Holden*, Jehovah's Witnesses, Portrait of a Contemporary Religious Movement*, Routledge, 2005, p.153

1914

[38] International Bible Students refers to the former name of Jehovah's Witnesses, before a major schism in 1909.

[39] NHS, National Statistics, *Smoking, drinking and drug use among young people in England in 2011*. Summary, July 2012

[40] 'Is the teen rebel a dying breed?' BBC NEWS Magazine, 2 October 2012

[41] BBC News, 'Cameron warns on child carer cuts,' D. Howard, http://www.bbc.co.uk/news/education-11757907

[42] http://www.carers.org/key-facts-about-carers

[43] Steven Pinker, *Better Angels of our Nature, The Decline of Violence in History and its Causes*, Penguin Group, 2011, p.117

[44] Pinker, p.125

[45] *The Story of England*, Michael Wood, 2010, p.185-189

[46] http://www.worldhunger.org/articles

[47] United Nations Development Program, China: Poverty and Social Inclusion
http://www.undp.org.cn/modules.php?op=modload&name=News&file=article&catid=10&sid=10

[48] http://www.aidswork.org/brief-history-of-aids/ (2010)

[49] John of Ephesus, p.74-75 quoted *In the Shadow of the Sword, The Battle for Global Empire and the End of the Ancient World*, Tom Holland, Pub. Little, Brown, 2012, p.270

[50] *In the Shadow of the Sword*, p.272-273

[51] 4 September 1665, *The Letters and Second Diary of Samuel Pepys*, Ed. R.G. Howarth, 1932, p.25

[52] http://www.umm.edu/news/releases/athens.htm#ixzz1qvgild2o

[53] Medical History, 1993, 37: 361-381, *Typhus and its Control in Russia, 1870-1940*, K. David Patterson

[54] CDC (Centers for Disease Control and Prevention),
http://www.cdc.gov/malaria/about/history/

[55] British Medical Journal, *Walcheren 1809: a medical catastrophe*, 18 December 1999; 319 (7225): 1642-1645.

[56] The latest report from UNAIDS (July 2012) reveals that the number of people dying from AIDS has been falling since 2005, from 2.3 million a year to 1.7million a year.

[57] 'Global burden of diseases and injuries for 291 causes in 21 regions,' 1990-2010, Murray *et al*, The *Lancet*, 2012

[58] The *Economist*, 'Global Health: Lifting the Burden,' December 15, 2012, p.77-78

[59] http://www.bgs.ac.uk/research/earthquakes/earthquakeActivity.html

[60] http://earthquake.usgs.gov/learn/topics/increase_in_earthquakes.php

[61] http://www.nytimes.com/2010/04/11/opinion/11musson.html?_r=0

[62] Proceedings of the National Academy of Sciences, *Global risk of big earthquakes has not recently increased*, January 17, 2012 vol. 109 no.3, p.717-721

[63] http://www.smh.com.au/environment/climate-change/north-america-sees-biggest-jump-in-climate-change-related-disasters-munichre-20121018-27s8u.html#ixzz2AKrIUtL8. October 8, 2012. See also Munich Re Press Release, October 17, 2012

[64] http://www.watchtower.org/e/19981101/article_01.htm

[65] *Worst Things People Have Done*, www.necrometrics.com

[66] *Genghis Khan – Biography*, Kallie Szczepa, http://asianhistory.about.com/od/profilesofasianleaders/p/GenghisKhanProf.htmnski

[67] *Better Angels,* p.132

Organization

[68] 'What Does the Bible *Really* Teach: Judgement Day – What Is It?' http://www.watchtower.org/e/bh/appendix_09.htm

[69] *Apply Yourself to Reading*, Watchtower Online Library

[70] The Kingdom Ministry School consists of a teaching program dealing with public speaking and door-to-door ministry, held every week at the Kingdom Hall.

[71] *Apply Yourself to Reading*, Watchtower Online Library, be p.21-p.26, par.5

[72] *Jehovah's Witnesses, Portrait of a Contemporary Religious Movement*, Andrew Holden, p.32,33

[73] *Totalitarianism*, C. Friedrich, Cambridge, MA: C, Harvard University Press, 1954

[74] *Discipline That Can Yield Peaceable Fruit,* www.watchtower.org/e/19880415/article_01.htm

[75] Watchtower April 15, 1988, 'Discipline That Can Yield Peaceable Fruit,' p.26-30

[76] http://www.independent.co.uk/news/uk/home-news/war-of-words-breaks-out-among-jehovahs-witnesses-2361448.html#disqus_thread

[77] *'Free Speech and Incitement to Religious Hatred.'* Text based on contributions from Brendan Larvor and Richard Norman following discussions by Humanist Philosophers' group, UK
See http://humanism.org.uk/about/humanist-philosophers/

[78] The Third Communist International, 4 March 1919, in Lenin: Collected Works, Moscow: Progress Publishers, 1997, xxix, 240-1

[79] *The Heart, Mind and Soul of Communism*, Dr. F. Schwarz
http://www.vlink.com/politics/index.php?subaction=showfull&id=1200896292&archive=&start_from=&ucat=&

[80] Stalin report to Seventeenth Party Congress ('Congress of the Victors') 26 January, 1934, in J.V. Stalin, *Works* (Moscow: Foreign Languages Publishing House, 1954) xiii, 203

[81] *Russia: A 1,000-Year Chronicle of the Wild East*, Martin Sixsmith, 2011, p.414

[82] Čermák, F., Cvrček, V., Schmiedtová, V. (eds): Slovník komunistické totality. Nakladatelství Lidové noviny, /Praha 2010. ISBN 978-80-7422-060-9

[83] *The Iron Curtain Kid*, Oliver Fritz, 2009, ISBN 978-1-4092-7725-5

[84] M. Heller and A. Nekrich, *Utopia in Power: The History of the Soviet Union from 1917 to the Present,* trans. M. Carlos (New York: Summit Books, 1986), p.286

Morality Revisited

[85]See 'Early Teen Marriage and Future Poverty,' Gordon B. Dahl, U.S. National Institute of Health National Library of Medicine (NIH/NLM), v.47(3) August 2010
'Teen marriage tied to higher risk for mental illness in women,' R. Nauert PhD, PsychCentral, Sept. 2011

[86] 'Is Teen Marriage a Solution?' Naomi Seiler, CLASP (Center for Law and Social Policy), April 2002

http://www.clasp.org/admin/site/publications_archive/files/0087.
pdf

See also, 'Religious Heritage and Teenage Marriage,' J.A.
Hammond, B.S. Cole, S.H. Beck, *Review of Religious Research,* Vol.
35, No. 2 (Dec., 1993), p.117-133, Pub. Religious Research
Association Inc.

[87] http://www.endcorporalpunishment.org/pages/progress/prohib_states.html

[88] Quoted in *Abolishing Corporal Punishment of Children,* Council of
Europe Publishing, Dec. 2007, p.14

[89] Darshak Sanghavi, 'Spank no more. Why are fewer parents
hitting their kids?' Dec. 2011
http://www.slate.com/articles/health_and_science/medical_exami
ner/2011/12/spanking_is_on_the_decline_why_.html

[90] Sources who are, or have been, Jehovah's Witnesses have asked
to remain anonymous.

[91] http://www.caller.com/photos/galleries/2010/aug/21/jehovahs-
witnesses-baptism/

[92] In the UK, convicted pedophiles are placed on the Sex Offenders
Register, which contains details of any individual convicted,
cautioned, or released from prison for a sexual offense against
children or adults. A convicted sex offender must not only register
initially when convicted or released from prison, but continue to
register on an annual basis.

[93] Quoted in Charles Freeman, *The Closing of the Western Mind:
The Rise of Faith and the Fall of Reason*

[94] Watchtower April 15, 1988, 'Discipline That Can Yield Peaceable
Fruit,' p.26-30

[95] Brochure, *'Who Are Doing Jehovah's Will Today?'* Lesson 6: 'How
Does Association With Fellow Christians Benefit Us?' Watchtower
Bible and Tract Society of New York, Inc. 2012, p.9

[96] http://www.youtube.com/watch?v=-_9kiS8U46E

[97] BBC Documentary, 'Close Up,' broadcast in south-west England,
circa 1996
http://www.youtube.com/watch?v=ST8iRJf783w

[98] Edward O. Wilson, *The Social Conquest of Earth*, Liveright Publishing Corporation, 2012, p.291-292

[99] Richard Dawkins, *The Selfish Gene*, 1976, p.ix

[100] Hebrews 13:8

[101] Copy of original document appended

[102] Year Book of Jehovah's Witnesses, 1934, p.135

[103] Copy of original document appended

[104]'Keep Your Eyes on the Prize,' *Sing to Jehovah,* Songbook of Jehovah's Witnesses, 2009

[105] Marc D. Hauser, *Moral Minds: How Nature Designed our Universal Sense of Right and Wrong*. Quoted in Richard Dawkins, *The God Delusion*, 2007, p.255

[106] 'America's Unfaithful Faithful,' *Time Magazine*, February 25, 2008

[107] *The Guardian*, 8 February, 2006

Reality

[108] A.C. Grayling, *The God Argument, the Case Against Religion and For Humanism*, Bloomsbury Publishing, 2013, p.257

[109] K.M. Kendric, 'Sheep Senses, Cognition and Capacity for Consciousness,' C.M. Dwyer (ed.), *The Welfare of Sheep*, Springer Science & Business Media B.V. 2008, p.144-145

[110] http://www.ted.com/talks/laura_carstensen_older_people_are_happier.html

[111] Edward O. Wilson, *The Social Conquest of Earth*, p.297

WATCH TOWER
BIBLE AND TRACT SOCIETY
PUBLISHERS OF THE BIBLE STUDENTS ASSOCIATION

Covering letter to the Declaration of Jehovah's Witnesses, June 25, 1933
Source: http//www.bible.ca/jw-hitler.htm#hitlerlett

Copy of part of the Declaration sent to Hitler in 1933. Note the section headed 'Juden' – Jews.

Recommended Reading & Other Media

Psychology, Philosophy and Social behavior

Letter to a Christian Nation by Sam Harris (2006)
An excellent little book that gives the best general overview of the problems inherent in religion

Better Angels of our Nature: A History of Violence and Humanity by Steven Pinker (2011)
This book, by psychologist Steven Pinker, is very good at setting the context for any discussion about the human condition, including religion. It is a detailed study of the decline in violence and improvement in public morality over the past few thousand years, together with an examination of the underlying causes of these trends.

The World until Yesterday by Jared Diamond (2012)
A study of tribal societies (based on contemporary 'pre contact' peoples), which illustrates how humans have lived through most of history. The book is good for gaining a better understanding of human nature. It also contains an excellent chapter on the origins of religion.

The Social Conquest of Earth by Edward O. Wilson (2012)
Edward Wilson has spent much of his career studying the social lives of ant, termite, and bee colonies, which has given him some useful insights into social behavior in human 'colonies' too. Once again, very good for gaining a better understanding of human nature. The chapter on the possible origins of religion is the best I have read.

Second Nature: The Inner Lives of Animals **by Jonathan P. Balcombe (2010)**
This is all about animal behavior and intelligence. It helps put humans into context with all the other species on earth, and demonstrates how egotistical it is to assume mankind is somehow a special exception, 'made in God's image.'

The Bonobo and the Atheist **by Frans de Waal (2013)**
A fascinating study of morality in primate society

The Moral Landscape **by Sam Harris (2010)**
An in-depth discussion of morality in the modern world.

The Antichrist **by Friedrich Nietzsche (1888)**
A nineteenth-century critique of Christianity. Occasionally unbalanced, but much of it still holds true.

Also Sprach Zarathustra **by Richard Strauss (1896)**
Orchestral Symphonic Poem that explores the release of mankind from the bondage of religion.

Alpine Symphony **by Richard Strauss (1915)**
Orchestral Symphony pointing to a superior philosophy (other than Christianity) for mankind, based on a proper appreciation of life as it is, rather than hankering for an afterlife. It suggests an alternative spirituality based on the an affinity with nature.

1984 by George Orwell (1949)

Classic novel set in a fictional dystopian state. There are so many parallels with contemporary life among Jehovah's Witnesses that it is difficult to believe that Orwell himself had not been a Witness at some point! Of course he hadn't, but this book shows that the Governing Body of Jehovah's Witnesses is using techniques that are well trodden by other totalitarian regimes of the past.

The Real North Korea: Life and Politics in the Failed Stalinist Utopia by Andrei Lankov (2013)

A remarkable account of the methods used by a totalitarian state, to keep their population in ignorance of the outside world.

Then They Came for Me by Maziar Bahari (2012)

An insight into life in a theocratic state – in this case, the Islamic Republic of Iran, where Maziar Bahari was imprisoned in 2009. There are strong parallels between the beliefs of the Iranian Revolutionary Guard and those of Jehovah's Witnesses.

A Thousand Splendid Suns by Khaled Hosseini (2007)

A novel that gives a vivid portrait of life in a theocratic state – in this case, Afghanistan under the Taliban. There are many parallels with Jehovah's Witness society, which is not surprising, given the links between Sharia Law and the Hebrew Scriptures.

The Handmaid's Tale by Margaret Attwood (1985)

Novel set in a fictional theocratic state of the future. A chilling portrait of a dystopian society, written especially from a

woman's point of view. Many parallels with contemporary
Jehovah's Witness society.

Brave New World by Aldous Huxley (1931)
Another classic novel set in a dystopian state with many
parallels to the Jehovah's Witness Organization.

The Iron Curtain Kid by Oliver Fritz (2009)
Autobiography capturing what it is like to grow up in
communist East Germany. A very humorous and lovable book,
which illustrates many parallels between the totalitarian East
German regime and that of the Governing Body of Jehovah's
Witnesses.

Russia: A 1000-Year Chronicle of the Wild East by Martin Sixsmith (2011)
A history of Russia, much of which is devoted to the Soviet era.
The chapters on the Soviet period illustrate the similarities
between the Soviet regime and that of the Governing Body of
Jehovah's Witnesses.

Lenin: A Biography: Life and Legacy by Dmitri Volkogonov (1995)
This author was a leading figure in the final days of the Soviet
regime. The book provides further insights into the structure of
totalitarian regimes, whether those of Jehovah's Witnesses or
the Soviet Union.

History

And Man Created God, Kings, Cults and Conquests at the Time of Jesus by Selina O'Grady (2012)

A wide-ranging study of religious beliefs at the time of Jesus, identifying the emergence of some of the familiar features of Christianity.

The Closing of the Western Mind: The Rise of Faith and the Fall of Reason by Charles Freeman (2002)

An excellent book that describes how Christians took control of the Roman Empire in the fourth century, and the serious consequences this had for the progress of science and its effect on morality.

In the Shadow of the Sword: The Battle for Global Empire and the End of the Ancient World by Tom Holland (2012)

A history of Christianity and Judaism in the fifth and sixth centuries, and how these religions eventually gave rise to Islam. Very good context for better understanding the three great monotheistic religions.

Agora, a feature film by Alejandro Amenabar, starring Rachel Weisz (2010)

A feature film rather than a book: Agora is set in fifth century Alexandria, and examines how the Christians took control of society, and what effect it had on science and public morality.

Jehovah's Witnesses

Jehovah's Witnesses: Portrait of a Contemporary Religious Movement by Andrew Holden (2002)

The only book I can recommend on Jehovah's Witnesses is this one by Andrew Holden. The author studied Jehovah's Witnesses for a PhD thesis, and his book, while being non-judgemental, has many useful insights.

The Bible

Cain by Joseph Saramago (2009)
Novel inspired by the book of Genesis, exploring various Bible stories seen through the eyes of Cain. Very good for stripping away the accretions of time and exposing familiar stories for what they really are.

Lost Christianities by Bart D. Ehrman (2003)
Essential for its information on the early forms of Christianity and beliefs. Also reveals the processes behind the formation of the New Testament.

Lost Scriptures: Books that did not make it into the New Testament by Bart D. Ehrman (2003)
An anthology of non-canonical writings from the early centuries after Christ.

Forged by Bart D. Ehrman (2011)
Contains compelling evidence to refute the authenticity of some of the Bible's books and passages of scripture included in the New Testament.

Science

The Greatest Show on Earth by Richard Dawkins (2009)
A good overall guide, setting out the evidence for evolution.

The Ancestor's Tale by Richard Dawkins (2005)
The history of life, right back to the beginning. Good for setting humanity in context.

My Beautiful Genome: Exposing our Genetic Future, One Quirk at a Time by Lone Frank (2011)

An exploration of the latest developments in human genetics, with new insights into what it means to be human.

The Incredible Human Journey by Alice Roberts (BBC) (2009)

A TV documentary exploring the journey of our earliest human ancestors out of Africa.

Humanism

For people who are concerned about morality, but who are troubled by the beliefs of religions, Humanism may be an option. The following links may be of interest to those wanting to know more:

British Humanist Association (BHA)
http://humanism.org.uk/

American Humanist Association (AHA)
http://www.americanhumanist.org/

5890033R00170

Printed in Great Britain
by Amazon.co.uk, Ltd.,
Marston Gate.